Customers
for
Keeps

8 powerful strategies to turn
customers into friends and
keep them forever

Lois K. Geller
President, Mason & Geller Direct Marketing

Adams Media Corporation
Avon, Massachusetts

Published by
Adams Media Corporation
57 Littlefield Street, MA 02322
www.adamsmedia.com

ISBN: 1-58062-561-4

Printed in the United States of America.

J I H G F E D C B A

Library of Congress Cataloging-in-Publication Data

Geller, Lois K.
Customers for keeps : 8 powerful friendship branding
strategies / Lois Geller.
Includes index.   p. cm.
ISBN 1-58062-561-4
1. Customer loyalty.

HF5415.525 .G45 2001
658.8'12—dc21   2001022155

Contents

Permissions

Figures 1.1, 1.2 The 10% coupon, "Indispensable travel dress" catalog excerpt, and accompanying comments used by permission of TravelSmith, P.O. Box 5729, Novato, CA, 94948.

Figure 2.1 Letter used by permission of 1-800-FLOWERS.

Figures 5.1, 5.2 Hanna Andersson catalog insert and page, as well as the accompanying comments, used by permission of Hanna Andersson, 1010 N.W. Flanders, Portland, OR, 97209.

Figure 5.3 "Spokeswrench" mailer and accompanying comments used by permission of Price Automotive, 168 North Dupont Highway, New Castle, DE, 19720.

Figure 5.4 The picture of the Taco Bell Chihuahua and accompanying comments used by permission of Taco Bell, 17901 Von Karman, Irvine CA, 92614.

Figure 5.5 "Born to Ship" ad and accompanying comments used by permission of Southwest Airlines, Love Field, P.O. Box 36611, Dallas, TX, 75235.

Figures 5.6, 5.7 "Flying Pig" catalog cover and the accompanying comments reprinted by permission of New Pig, One Pork Avenue, Tipton, PA, 16684.

Figure 6.1 The postcard of the "Farm Fresh Five" and accompanying comments used by permission of Stew Leonard's, Norwalk, CT.

Figure 7.1 "Diabetes Weight Loss System" advertisement and accompanying comments used by permission of the Marketing Development Group, 1200 Potomac Street, NW, Washington, D.C., 20007.

Figure 7.2 The Mark McGwire cards ad and accompanying comments used by permission of Mr. Joe England, 48 Myrtle Avenue, Westport, CT, 06880.

Figures 7.3, 7.4 The DMA mailer and accompanying text used by permission of httprint, 2351 Powell Street, Suite 501, San Francisco, CA, 94133.

Figures 7.6, 7.7, 7.8 1-800-PETFOOD coupon, ad, and the accompanying comments by Ms. Lisa Roland used by permission of Everyday Media, 461 Park Avenue South, New York, NY, 10016.

Figure 10.1 The Lillian Vernon ad and accompanying comments used by permission of the Lillian Vernon Corporation, One Theall Road, Rye, NY, 10580.

Figure 10.2 The Lands' End "We'll knock ourselves out for you" page and accompanying comments used by permission of Lands' End, Inc., 1 Lands' End Lane, Dodgeville, WI, 53595.

Figures 10.3, 10.4 The pages from "We Want You to Feel Good Inside" booklet and accompanying comments used by permission of Stonyfield Farm, Ten Burton Drive, Londonderry, NH, 03053.

Figures 11.1, 11.2 The FSI for Starbucks coffee and accompanying comments used by permission of Starbucks, P.O. Box 34067, Seattle, WA, 98124-1067.

Figures 11.3, 11.4 "Angelic Herald" newsletter page, Fairyland cruise announcement, and accompanying comments used by permission of Kirks Folly, 389 Fifth Avenue, New York, NY, 10016.

Figures 11.5, 11.6 "What do we have to do to get you back" card and accompanying comments used by permission of Doubleday Direct, Inc., 401 Franklin Avenue, Garden City, NY, 11530.

Preface

There are those who pass like ships in the night
Who meet for a moment, then sail out of sight
With never a backwards glance of regret
Folks we know briefly then quickly forget

Then there are those friends who sail together
Through quiet waters and stormy weather
Helping each other through joy and through strife
And they are the kind that give meaning to life.

—author unknown

I've been thinking about Friendship Branding for many years now. The idea really started more than ten years ago, when I was creating direct marketing campaigns for Ford of Canada. I wanted to change our communications style. I thought that the letters we mailed should sound like they were coming from real human beings, not corporate headquarters. I found that I certainly responded better to advertisements and promotions and direct mail that spoke directly to me, that sounded like something a real person, and not a stuffed shirt, would say. I responded to communications that had a little zip, a bit of an edge, and a distinctive personality.

Yes, personality—a personality that gave me some idea of who I was dealing with. Why don't I like to get letters from stuffed shirts? Because stuffed shirts have a personality that I can't relate to, and they're not people I would choose to have as my friends.

That's when I made the connection. There are thousands and thousands of products, services, companies and brands in the world. How do I choose the ones I buy and the ones I don't? When I stopped to think about it, I realized that there are some brands toward which I naturally gravitate. And those are brands to which I can personally relate. They represent something to me. They represent trust and loyalty, sharing and caring, security and understanding. They know me and appreciate what I bring to their table. They are like friends to me.

Turns out that *the very attributes I look for in friends are the same ones I look for in brands.*

This book is filled with examples of companies that I've studied, ones that I like, ones that provide excellent examples of Friendship Branding. Friendship Branding is about thinking of your company in a human way. Those are the companies and brands that build loyalty over time. It's about ways that your brand can deliver distinctive consumer satisfaction and build long-term relationships with each and every person who buys from you. It's about building brands that people respect and enjoy.

The purpose of this book is to encourage you to experiment with breakthrough ideas. Study the brands featured in these pages and see the great strides that are being made in the way people think, and not by spending millions and millions of dollars in new advertising strategies. *Friendship*

Branding can be practiced successfully by anyone, regardless of the size of your company or the product or service you sell.

After interviewing many marketing experts and company owners and doing my own consumer research with the Geller Branding Survey, I read every branding book I could find. I was looking for a book I could recommend to my clients and use in my class at New York University that would simplify the process of building a brand. I discovered that there are all kinds of complicated theories on this subject. But after I read them, I could barely recall what these authors had said. Even though some of them were full of charts and numbers and scientific "analysis" of what goes into branding success, they were all missing one thing: the simple human factor, which gets one person buying from another person.

So I decided to write this book, *Customers for Keeps*, about branding and what it means to me. Branding is not about a logo, or packaging, or pricing, or extensions, or position, although all these things are part of it. It is about friendship, and about the companies that understand how to make friends and keep them over time.

I hope this book is the beginning of a friendship between you and me. When I wrote my first book, *RESPONSE! The Complete Guide to Profitable Direct Marketing,* I was thrilled with how many people wrote to me, e-mailed me, and even visited our offices after reading the book. That is the best part of the book-writing process, so I hope I will hear from you, too. Just fill out the form at the end of this book and mail it to me. I welcome your questions and comments, and your own Friendship Branding examples.

Good luck. Make your company a Friendship Brand!

Acknowledgments

This book has been a wonderful collaboration experience from the start. It began with my ideas on "Friendship Branding" and how we make the process build relationships between our clients and their customers.

While speaking about Friendship Branding at a conference, I met Martha Jewett, who liked the idea. Thanks to Martha, a great literary agent (*www.marthajewett.com*), Adams Media easily agreed to publish it.

I am grateful to Jennifer Praeger, who helped assemble and "put together" the mountain of materials I gathered each day on my desk. She was there through revisions and helped make the process fun! I also enlisted the creative mind of Harvey Ardman, who helped to organize chapters and contributed his own ideas, and his sense of humor.

I am also grateful to Pepper Huff, who adds his own Friendship Branding style to whatever he does, both artistically and personally. And a big thanks to everyone else at the agency; you make our days productive and fun.

Also, this book and all the great work we do at the office would not be possible without the help of Michael McCormick. Thank you, Michael.

We do great work because we have amazing clients and friends especially the gang at American Express—Murray Miller,

Pat Hurlock, Yvonne Manning and the wonderful Liz Bieler; Barbara Hanson from Thomas Register; Lee Epstein from Mailman; and Renee Harris from New York University.

Then there is my own best friend, Andrea Nierenberg, who gives new meaning to the word *friendship*. I am always amazed at how much I learn from her and the value of our long talks.

Most important, I thank my family for all their support. My mom—Regina Kaufman—has always delighted in the things I do. I'll always remember the great fuss she made over my school essays! And my dad, who passed away last year, also encouraged me every step of the way; he will always be an inspiration to me.

My son, Paul Geller, and his wife, Joan, are the lights of my life, and it is to them that I dedicate this book. They have brought me joy, positive thinking, and love, and I cherish every moment with them.

Special Acknowledgment to Charles Mason

Charlie Mason is my partner in Mason & Geller. He is the owner of a number of excellent communications companies including Mason & Madison Advertising & Public Relations, Mason & Kichar Recruitment, Wide Eye Marketing, and net-Feat, all of which are dedicated to innovative strategy and flawless execution in creating intimate bonds between our clients and their customers.

—Lois K. Geller

Introduction

Friendship is the hardest thing in the world to explain. It's not something you learn in school. But if you haven't learned the meaning of friendship, you haven't really learned anything.

—*Muhammad Ali*

This is the first book to tear down the standard definition of branding—creating a physical image and mental association of a product or service in the customer's mind—and create a new definition for the new millennium and the new consumer. The new definition describes a brand as a living, evolving experience between two "people": the company and the customer. It is the only book to show how to find and keep customers *by treating them like friends.*

Customers for Keeps: Eight Powerful Friendship Branding Strategies will show you how to do the following:

- Create and maintain a memorable, effective brand, no matter how large or small the company.
- Redefine the brand as an experience rather than an image.

- Relate to customers as you would to your best friends, using the principles and "rituals" of friendship to create strong, long-lasting relationships.
- Market to customers most likely to buy your products or services.
- Improve listening skills in order to encourage and respond to valuable customer feedback.
- Inspire trust, respect, and loyalty in customers.
- Repair "broken" relationships so that they are stronger than ever.

The business world has been talking about relationship marketing—developing a one-to-one connection with customers—for years now. This book picks up where relationship marketing leaves off. It's about how the simple concept of treating customers like friends can extend a company's brand and encourage customers to remain loyal. It's less about what a company needs to do to market its products than about *how* they need to do it to be successful. There are so many companies out there marketing "me-too" products. At times, it seems impossible to tell one apparel brand or one cola drink from another.

The reason the Friendship Branding concept is so unique is that it goes beyond relationship and one-to-one marketing, beyond branding itself, and into the next era of marketing evolution. Friendship Branding shifts the focus from describing a brand as an idea and image to defining a brand as a life experience.

If you take nothing else away from this book, take this: Friendship Branding means treating your customers as friends—not "as if" they were friends, not so they *think* they're being treated like friends, but with genuine feelings of friendship.

And it means keeping these friendly feelings in mind in every aspect of your business, including design, production, marketing, sales, and service. It means that every company employee should understand the idea and be on board.

At its heart, Friendship Branding is more an attitude than a technique. And it's an easy attitude to adopt, if you think about the role your customers play in your life and well-being, and that of your company and your employees, as well as their families. Yes, customers are hard to please sometimes. Yes, they can be demanding. Yes, they can be fickle. But whatever trouble they give you, they're worth it. And if you and your employees truly grasp that idea, your actions will automatically reflect your understanding.

I know—and your customers know—that you can't possibly be on a first-name basis with all of them. Your company may deal with millions of customers. But even some of the largest companies manage to create the warm emotional bond with their customers that leads to long-term loyalty.

The story that follows is a great example of Friendship Branding:

A few years ago, my wonderful parents were celebrating their 65th (!) wedding anniversary. The party was to be held at 7:00 P.M. at the Alexander Hotel in Miami. I flew down from New York, arriving at 2:00 P.M. so that I'd have enough time to help them get dressed and ready for the party.

This was such a special occasion. The whole family was going to be there. I'd shopped for weeks and found the perfect dress—purple silk. I bought new shoes to go with it.

I'd taken extra care to pack them both into a suit bag and planned to take it onto the plane with me.

When I got to the airport, however, I was told that the flight was overbooked and that I'd have to check my luggage through. Against my better judgment, I did.

Of course, you know what happened next. I waited at the luggage carousel as everyone else's bags spun around. I was just starting to panic when I saw my bag come tumbling down the chute. As I picked it up, I realized that the underside was in shreds, my beautiful purple dress in tatters!

Apparently, the bag had somehow gotten caught in the conveyor belt. I was in tears as I hurried to the Lost Luggage counter. The longer I stood in line, the more I was aching for a fight. I finally reached the counter and told my story to the woman behind it. I explained about my parents' party, that it was that evening and that I bought the dress and shoes specifically for this occasion. I couldn't wait for her to give me a form to fill out and tell me to send it in for reimbursement.

Instead, she asked, "What can we do for you?"

I told her the total cost of everything I had in the bag. She didn't ask me for proof. She told me to wait a moment. She went into the back, spoke to her supervisor, and came back with a check in her hand.

"Nothing can replace your lovely dress or make up for your aggravation," she said. "But I can give you this check. And if you'll be patient for just another five minutes, we'll get Jimmy in the back to drive you to the store of your choice so you can purchase another outfit. He'll wait for you outside and then drive you to your parents' house. We don't want anything to spoil this night for you."

And that's just what happened.

This is a true story. It was the kindest thing anyone other than a personal friend has ever done for me. And it was done by the people at American Airlines. I may take my frequent flyer points for granted, and I appreciate the fact that they once got me a hotel room when my plane was canceled, but I know that that is standard company policy. However, their act of kindness that day in Miami is one I will never forget—and it is a perfect example of Friendship Branding. *And it is an example of the Friendship Branding technique that this book will explain.*

In *Customers for Keeps*, I'm going to tell you exactly how to master all the stages of a Friendship Branding, and how to apply all of these Friendship Branding techniques to your company, your products, and your services. You'll discover how to make the subtle changes that spell the difference between one-time buyers and lifelong customers.

And in the process, I hope we become friends as well. Why? Because I like to practice what I preach.

We are advertised by our loving friends.
        —*William Shakespeare*

Chapter One

What Is Friendship Branding?

Friendship Branding is a method of creating a warm emotional bond between buyers and sellers, between manufacturers and consumers, between stores and customers, between businesses doing business with each other—in short, between any two parties to a transaction. And absolutely nothing—not low prices, not high quality, not broad selection, not easy availability, not even high marks from consumer magazines—makes customers more loyal to a product, store, or service provider than a warm emotional bond.

Friendship Branding is as different from conventional branding as friends are different from acquaintances. I care about my friends, and you care about yours. We go out of our way for our friends. We tolerate their faults. We're happy when we're with them.

How do friends act toward each other? Well, think of your friends. Think of what you want from them. Think of what they want from you. Think of the ways in which friends are special to each other:

- They do favors for each other.
- They give each other priority.
- They treat each other with good will.
- They watch each other's backs and protect each other.
- They make allowances for each other's shortcomings.
- They try to spend time together.
- They are considerate of each other.
- They are openly affectionate with each other.

Bottom line: They *care* for one another.

Human beings form friendships. They hit it off and start giving to each other, with no immediate prospect of getting back anything in return. With luck, it becomes mutual. And you know what? It lasts . . . and lasts . . . and lasts, sometimes a lifetime.

Classic Friendship Branding Techniques

Friendship is an important part of our personal lives, and it enriches everything we do. The phrase *Friendship Branding* is new, but some of its component parts have been around since the dawn of human commerce. Expanding on this base is what makes Friendship Branding a powerful way to do business.

"Wash Your Windshield, Ma'am?"

You don't hear the term *service station* much anymore, because you're a lot more likely to get gas at a *self*-service station than at a gas station with a friendly, eager attendant. But once upon a time, "Service Stations" was a Yellow Pages category, and that's where you'd look if you wanted to find a place to gas up the family car, or buy batteries and tires, or get the oil changed. And in those days, if someone pulled into a service station—even someone from out of town—he or she got the windshield wiped and the oil and tire pressures checked, and never had to touch the greasy gas pump. He or she got service. And that's an essential piece of Friendship Branding.

Friendship Branding service goes beyond customers' expectations. For instance, my colleague Julia saw an ad for TravelSmith's "Indispensable Black Dress" in a magazine and called to request a catalog. When the catalog arrived a few days later, it contained a coupon for 10 percent off her first order (see Figures 1.1 and 1.2).

Julia called the toll-free number to order four items. No problem with the first three, but the raincoat she wanted was out of stock. She expressed her disappointment, as she wanted the coat for an upcoming trip. The operator asked Julia for her date of departure. She then looked up the exact date the products were expected and offered to upgrade Julia's shipment to two-day air—at no additional charge—so that it would arrive in time for her trip.

That's excellent service. But that's not all. Two days later, Julia realized she also needed a pair of shorts. She called TravelSmith again. The operator she spoke to (not the same one as

MACHINE-WASHABLE   WRINKLE-RESISTANT

OUR "INDISPENSABLE" TRAVEL FABRIC: SUPPLEX/LYCRA KNIT

Our Indispensable Black Travel Dress owes its indispensability to its fabric, one of your smartest choices for travel. Supplex®/Lycra® knit combines elegance, comfort, and easy care into one packable, wrinkle-resistant blend. Soft and natural to the eye and hand, it drapes beautifully and has just enough stretch for resilience and comfort. On the road or at home, you'll especially appreciate the way Supplex®/Lycra knit can be washed and dried quickly, by hand or machine, saving you the expense and delay of dry-cleaning.

THE INDISPENSABLE BLACK TRAVEL DRESS™
Supplex® Knit Elegantly Defies Wrinkles

Fashions come and go, but the "little black dress" never fails you. Dress it up with pearls, dress it down with flats: The look is timeless, understated, and always fitting. Our Indispensable Black Travel Dress lets you take that versatile elegance on the road. We've made it of a fluid Supplex®/Lycra® knit – a superb, slightly stretchy blend that is impervious to wrinkles – and given it a classic, easy-to-wear silhouette that looks good on absolutely everyone. No zippers, no buttons, no fuss: Just slip it on over your head. The jewel neckline can be accessorized with scarves or a favorite pendant for evenings on the town; the empire waist and slightly flaring skirt give every figure a flattering line. Choose the graceful below-the-calf length or the new above-the-knee style; either version can be rolled up and tucked into a corner of your bag, leaving you prepared for any occasion, anywhere on the planet. Made in USA. In *Black* and now available in *Midnight*. **Regular or Petite** sizes XS(2–4), S(6–8), M(10–12), L(14–16), XL(18–20).
Indispensable Black Dress™ #5183 **$99**
Short Indispensable Black Dress™ #5128 **$89**

LONG-SLEEVE INDISPENSABLE BLACK DRESS™

Equally as elegant, but more appropriate for cooler weather and conservative locales, this classic dress has long sleeves, a mock turtleneck, and a flattering empire waist. The fabric is a fluid blend of Supplex® nylon and a little Lycra® for gentle, shape-holding stretch. Slight flare allows a pleasing drape and room to stride. Graceful below-the-calf length. Made in USA. In *Black* or *Midnight*. **Regular or Petite** sizes XS(2–4), S(6–8), M(10–12), L(14–16), XL(18–20).
Long-Sleeve Indispensable Black Dress™ #5184 **$109**

13

Figure 1.1 TravelSmith's Indispensable Black Travel Dress is a big draw for many first-time customers.

OUTFITTER TO THE WORLD'S TOP TRAVEL COMPANIES
60 LEVERONI COURT • NOVATO, CA 94949 • 1-800-950-1600

Welcome to a new world of traveling comfortable, traveling smart, and traveling light.
Please use the coupon below to take 10% off your first order!

World Travelers:

Thank you for requesting our catalog. We're happy to send it to you along with our
Global Outfitting Guide. The Guide will help you prepare for your journey with detailed packing
lists and no-nonsense advice for all kinds of trips.

Every product in our catalog has been chosen for its "travelworth." That means each has been
thoroughly field-tested to be utterly reliable, lightweight, easy to pack and easy to care for on the road.

Our telephone staff are all trained outfitting specialists who will happily assist you in preparing
for your trip. Call us at 1-800-950-1600 and they'll help make your journey the best it can be.

We are eager to please you. That requires gaining your confidence and supplying you with the best
travel gear available anywhere in the world. We also know we have to respond to your requests
immediately and reliably. So be assured that we will ship any order you place the same day it is received.

Perhaps more important is our guarantee. Every product in our catalog has been carefully selected to
please you. If you are unhappy with what you order for any reason – or for no reason at all –
return it for a full refund or exchange, whichever you like.

Clip this coupon and enclose it with your first TravelSmith order, or give the coupon number to our
outfitter when you call. It allows you to subtract 10% off the total of your order (before tax and
shipping charges), no matter how much you order, if you order by the date shown on the coupon.

It's the first thing we can do to help you with your upcoming trip! Bon Voyage!

Chuck Slaughter   Scott Sklar

SAVE 10%

TRAVELSMITH

EARLY ORDER COUPON 391519   APR 0 5 1999

SAVE 10%

TAKE 10% OFF YOUR ORDER

If you send this coupon in (or call) before

Please clip this coupon and enclose it with your first order from TravelSmith.
If you order by telephone, please mention the coupon number above to the Operator.
This coupon entitles you to 10% off the total price of merchandise
from your first TravelSmith order (before adding taxes and shipping).

Not combinable with other offers or discounts. Good for one use only. Thanks.

24 HOURS • 1-800-950-1600

Figure 1.2   First-time customers get packing guides, advice for traveling,
and an added bonus of 10% off their merchandise.

before) asked her if she needed them for her upcoming trip. Apparently, the first operator had made a notation on the database. When Julia said yes, he upgraded her to two-day air shipment, for no extra charge. Julia started raving about TravelSmith before she received any merchandise! She now buys all her travel items from them, and keeps introducing her new "friend" to her friends, who are all becoming TravelSmith customers.

"This Blush Would Suit You Perfectly."

The makeup consultant is the department store makeup counter employee who makes customers into clients by establishing a personal relationship with them. The consultant does this by first spending time with a customer to help her figure out her makeup needs, then keeping her informed—through phone calls or even letters—of new products that she might like. The best of these people become friends of their clients rather than department store sales associates. They provide a personal touch, which is an essential element in Friendship Branding.

The Unexpected Gift

Good customers, like good friends, like to be appreciated. Some companies have always known that and thus offer their customers sales specials and other goodies. Some new companies have also caught on. For example, I buy lots of books from Amazon.com. In one of my orders, they included a beautiful insulated plastic coffee cup, emblazoned with Amazon.com's name and logo. I hadn't asked for it. I hadn't expected it. It just came, with a nice little note of appreciation. I'd long thought of myself as a loyal customer, but when a company actually gives me something useful, well, someone would have to put a gun to my head to get me to shop elsewhere. Customer appreciation is another key part of Friendship Branding.

Help When Needed

Once upon a time—well, it seems that way—Wallach's, a New York haberdashery on Fifth Avenue and 45th Street, offered a service to everyone in the city: If you had a button that popped—a coat button, a collar button, a jacket button—all you had to do was take it downstairs to their tailoring department, and they'd sew it back on while you waited, no charge. Didn't matter where you bought the item. Didn't matter if you were a Wallach's customer. Didn't even matter if you'd lost the button— they'd find a look-alike. Now, although they made the repair promptly, you always had a few minutes to look around while you waited. Maybe you saw a pair of shoes you just had to have, or a sweater, or a couple of silk ties. Maybe you just got the opportunity to see the quality of Wallach's clothing. When the tailor walked out with the button back in place, you couldn't help but have warm feelings toward the store and resolve to drop in the next time clothing was on your shopping list.

Happy Birthday, Dear Adam

I don't know what fast-food chain thought of it first, but I do know that McDonald's, Burger King, and Pizza Hut, and probably a bunch more, offer people—especially children—a free meal on their birthdays. This is a sure way to build customer loyalty, not to mention parental gratitude. It's not terribly expensive, especially compared to the amount of business it can generate, and it's easy to manage, with a registration book and some postcards. In fact, you don't have to be a restaurant to pull it off. The technique can be used by a variety of businesses and products. Remembering something personal about the customer, something that makes him or her smile—that's another Friendship Branding technique.

It's Like Having a Relative in the Business

The following story, told to me by my cousin, illustrates a unique and very powerful way to make loyal customers. About six months ago, he walked into a clothing store—one of a chain of clothing stores in the Florida region—and bought a suit that the store altered for him at no charge. A few months later, he went on a diet and lost thirty pounds. He took the suit back, and the store altered it again—still no charge. In the next few months, he took off another twenty pounds. He went back with the suit. They decided it couldn't be altered properly, so they *gave* him a new suit of comparable value. Turns out, this is the chain's policy: free alterations for the life of the garment and a replacement if the alterations don't do the trick. By the way, my cousin is still losing weight, and he's thinking of going back for more alterations. It wouldn't surprise me if he bought a couple more suits . . . and sweaters . . . and jackets . . . and shirts . . . and ties. That replacement suit made him a customer for life.

And It's Yours for Free!

One of the problems with high-tech goodies is that they're constantly being outdated by something with more speed, more memory, more features, greater capability, better design, or something else that makes you sorry you bought the old one and wish you had the new one. Lots of companies—for example, Sony, Dell, and Hewlett-Packard—actually depend on this phenomenon. Whatever they're selling today, they have a better one on the way, and it will turn whatever you're buying now into outdated trash. But a few firms don't follow this practice. I've bought several software programs that give you the next few versions of the program for free. I think that's both generous and understanding—and those are two more facets of Friendship Branding.

Friendship Branding is the conscious application of all these techniques and more, with the aim of creating a warm emotional bond between buyer and seller and between product and customer that leads to long-term loyalty. It is a philosophy not simply of branding but of doing business.

Conventional branding is aimed at specific demographic targets. It conveys information about pricing, quality, and/or features. Friendship Branding does *not* replace any of these strategies. It is an umbrella under which all other branding strategies can fit.

What Can Friendship Branding Do for You?

I wish I could guarantee you that Friendship Branding will transform your business, that your customers will double and your stock price quadruple. But there are no guarantees in this business, except perhaps for this one: If you don't adopt Friendship Branding in one way or another, you're going to find yourself fighting off competitors who do, and chances are you'll wind up losing market share.

Even if Friendship Branding doesn't add a dime to your bottom line (but it will), your company will benefit from it, and in more ways than one:

- Your employees will have a new and clearer sense of purpose.
- Your employees will feel that they're engaged in something greater—and perhaps better—than just making money.
- Your employees will feel they're making an important contribution to the happiness and satisfaction of other people, which, according to practically every religion, is good for the soul.
- Your employees will be proud to say where they work. We all know some examples: "I'm a distributor for Ben and Jerry's," someone says. And everyone else says, "Hey, that must be a great company to work for," and is suitably impressed. Ben and Jerry's has proved itself through Friendship Branding in its focus on natural ingredients and its community involvement. Or take L. L. Bean. People who work there are proud of their company's excellent reputation for customer service.
- Your employees will spread the good word. When employees feel a part of your Friendship Branding endeavor, they'll talk about it with relatives and friends, magnifying your efforts.
- Your employees will feel a greater loyalty to the company, because they respect and support its aims and goals.

But this is all just a byproduct of Friendship Branding. The greatest potential lies with your customers. If what you say and what you do convinces *them* that Friendship Branding is the real thing, they'll be loyal to your company, its products, and its services until their last credit card expires.

Today, most new customers are replacements for customers that have moved on. And we know that it costs more to replace a customer than to keep one you have. But Friendship Branding, if you implement it thoroughly and sincerely, can reduce the fall-off rate so that new customers are more often *additions* than replacements. It can permanently increase your customer base.

Friendship Branding can also create a vast army of fans, of unpaid sales people who will, for years to come, spread the good word about your company and your products or services. I know this because I'm one such fan. I constantly talk about the companies, products, and services that I like or that treat me well. And the better they treat me, the more I talk about them.

For example, one cold winter day, I went looking for my favorite pair of gloves, a pair of shearling-lined beauties I'd bought from L. L. Bean a few years earlier. I practically turned the house upside down, but all I could find was the left one.

A few weeks later, I happened to be in Freeport, Maine, and I'd remembered to take my one remaining glove with me. I went to a service desk at the giant L. L. Bean store.

"Do you still sell these?" I asked, hoping I could buy a new pair.

"Sure do," the clerk told me. "Do you need another pair?"

"Yes," I said. "I've lost the mate to this one."

"Hmm," said the clerk. She took the glove, checked the size, and told me she'd be right back. And sure enough, in a few minutes she returned—with a replacement for my missing right glove.

"Great!" I said. "How much?"

"No charge," she said with a smile.

I think I've told that story at least a dozen times since it happened. And you probably won't be surprised to know that I have a closet full of L. L. Bean jackets, slacks, and, yes, gloves. And you know what? So do my friends. If you multiply this kind of good will by a thousand customers, you can build a business on it, which is exactly what L. L. Bean has done.

How Hard Is It to Adopt and Apply Friendship Branding?

Friendship Branding is not particularly complicated, and it's not particularly expensive. You don't have to be a rocket scientist to understand the concept or to apply it to whatever goods or services you may be selling.

But that doesn't mean it's easy to adopt and apply. It's not. It requires an attitude change—not just from you but from your entire company and all of its employees. And this change must start at the top of your organization and be adopted by employees at all levels.

What kind of attitude change are we talking about? How can a company—a nonhuman institution, a legal entity, a group of buildings filled with a bunch of nameless, faceless employees—hope to establish a warm emotional bond with the flesh-and-blood people who are its customers? How can a corporation, a store, a service company win from its customers the kind of loyalty they reserve for friends?

There is a way. It won't always work, and it usually won't work quickly. But it is the key to winning customer loyalty: You must treat the customer exactly the way friends treat friends. That's the attitude change behind Friendship Branding: to truly, deeply, madly treat customers the way friends treat friends.

To adopt this attitude, you have to shelve, or at least draw back from, some others, including some deeply ingrained ways of thinking. For example, "making the sale" can no longer be your sole motive. Would that be your sole motive if you were selling something to a good friend? No. You'd think of his interests as well as your own.

You can't myopically focus on making a profit. Maybe friends should pay full price, but they should also get their money's worth.

You can't cut corners on quality. You wouldn't want to sell something substandard to a friend, would you?

You can't abandon your customer after the sale. Would you do that to a friend? Of course not.

You can't treat your best customers like everyone else. Your best friends get priority, don't they?

The odd thing is that when you start thinking of your customer as your friend, all of this falls into place quite naturally. But the attitude change can't be of the lip service variety. If it's anything less than sincere, it won't work. In fact, it will damage your relationship with the customer.

The other day I found myself eating at a crowded restaurant. The service was glacial and the food was barely edible. "Everythin' okay, hun?" The waitress asked over her shoulder in passing, as she swooped by. "Yeah, sure," I said, clenching my fists. I didn't feel guilty leaving a small tip, because phony friendliness is worse than none at all. That's true in personal relationships, and it's true when money changes hands. Phony friendliness breeds suspicion.

Yes, I know changing attitudes isn't easy. But your customers truly deserve your friendship. They're putting food on the table. And if you treat them right, they'll keep doing it for years to come.

So now you have a better idea of what Friendship Branding is and how it can affect your company. (Applying what you've learned, that is, creating a company that embraces Friendship Branding, is an eight-stage process that we'll take a look at in Chapter 4.)

Chapter Summary

- A brand is a living, evolving experience between two entities: the company and the customer.

- The reason people are loyal to a particular brand, product, or company is that they can depend on it. If you want to make customers loyal, make yourself someone worthy of loyalty. Put yourself in your customer's place. How do you like to be treated? What makes you feel special?

- The basis of Friendship Branding is to relate to customers as you would a good friend. It's especially important to be a good listener and work through any difficulties. You must be willing to do whatever it takes to keep the relationship strong.

- Friendship Branding has to be incorporated into a company's vision and processes. It has to start at the top of an organization and be adopted by employees at all levels. In your own organization, identify the employees who deal directly with customers and empower them to use Friendship Branding techniques.

- Never underestimate the power of word of mouth. In fact, the Internet has added an entirely new dimension to the dissemination of information about products and services. There is the online discussion board method, which is devoted to user opinions, and there's e-mail, another new avenue through which people can express their likes and dislikes.

- If you think you can't afford to implement the kinds of strategies reviewed, think again. You can't afford NOT to! Whether it's an unexpected gift or an offer of free postage and handling, you have to be committed to customer retention and plan to allocate resources—because it pays high returns.

- Friendship Branding benefits your company employees in many ways and helps them to stay motivated. In particular, it gives everyone a clearer sense of purpose and the feeling that he or she is contributing to other people's satisfaction and happiness.

- The results from our Geller Branding Survey are revealing. Over half of the respondents said that they would, in fact, like to receive more catalogs. These customers want to hear more about the products and services being offered, not less. You never get tired of hearing from your friends—the people you really like! In addition, these customers said that the most important factors in staying loyal to a particular brand are (1) consistent quality, (2) customer service, and (3) price. The way customers are treated—in terms of consistently high-quality products and responsive customer service—is what really counts. Price came in last of the three!

*Life's truest happiness is found in friendships
we make along the way.*

—Unknown

Chapter Two

Making Friends

Not so long ago, we were all quite comfortable dealing with companies that treated us exactly like everyone else, companies that had about as much personality and character as the average high-rise apartment building.

We liked things that way. We were in awe of huge institutions that had been around forever and that were famous for turning out reasonably reliable—and totally identical—products by the tens of millions. General Electric comes to mind, and Sears, and Procter & Gamble.

At my house, for example, when the Sears catalog arrived, it was an event. We kids were eager to see it, but we didn't have a chance until Mom had studied the clothing section and Dad had gone through hardware thoroughly, circling what he hoped he could buy. But what was Sears to us? It was more like a government agency than anything else—the quartermaster corps for the civilian population.

We actually liked the impersonal treatment we got from these giant companies. It was kind of reassuring. It helped us see ourselves as equal to everyone else, as belonging to a community of similar folks with similar lifestyles, similar needs, similar problems with similar solutions. Even our middle-class homes were identical: living room with one picture window, one couch, one television (watch *Leave It to Beaver* reruns and you'll see what I mean). We carried our credit cards around in our wallets and purses like proof of membership.

But that was then, when prosperity was still something of a novelty. It was a time when the cornucopias in our supermarkets and malls still seemed a bit miraculous, when having not only everything you needed but also practically everything you wanted was still so new that it didn't occur to us there could be more.

Those days are gone and their memory is fading. Now we're all material girls, or boys. Whatever impressed us or our parents about the American system of mass production and distribution we now take for granted. We want more.

More what?

Well, it's no longer good enough to merely feel equal to our friends and neighbors. "Keeping up with the Joneses" doesn't win us any points. I want *more* than the Joneses, and I'll bet you do, too. We want to impress them with our taste and shopping smarts. We want to dazzle 'em with our possessions. We buy things that confirm and proclaim our individuality, our status, even our worth as people.

So much for mass production.

When I was a college student, we had a motto: "Don't fold, mutilate, or spindle." That slogan was printed on IBM computer punch cards because they wouldn't go through the machine if they were damaged. Well, we wanted our schools to treat us just as carefully—like individuals.

Now we've grown up, and we want the same from the whole world—not just from our friends and relatives but from everyone we come in contact with, including Macy's, Exxon, American Express, and all the rest. If they don't treat us as individuals, we're insulted.

I have often thought about branding as being a strategy for major companies like Coca-Cola, Procter & Gamble, Disney, Apple, and Dell. Why large companies? Because they have the resources to spend millions of dollars on advertising, promotion, and public relations that will "get the word out" about their products. We're used to equating the word *brand* with the word *big*.

Years ago we had to respect the big brands because we had no choice. I remember living in Boston and waiting three weeks to get a phone installed. Sure I could complain, but so what? I didn't have the leverage of threatening to take my business elsewhere, so the phone company could simply say "Sorry" and take their sweet time anyway. There were only three credit cards to choose from. No one dared complain about high interest rates; it was pay what they asked or go without.

Those huge monoliths still exist in some cases, but we don't have to play their game anymore. There are too many other options. When they were the only players, they could afford to treat customers poorly. Now, every brand has the problem of customer loyalty.

This morning, I had to call my local telephone service provider about my account. When the representative and I had finished our business, she asked, "Would you say I have treated you like a valued customer?" I laughed and said, "Yes, of course."

But then I thought about it. That question, which evidently is now part of the routine whenever a customer calls, was aimed at two people:

- First, it was aimed at the phone company representative. Someone at the phone company figured that if she knew she'd have to ask it at the end of the conversation, she might treat the customer with increased care and attention.
- Second, it was aimed at me—and at you. It was designed to show us that the phone company *cares* about how we are treated during the course of a routine business call.

The question was contrived and slightly ridiculous, but it was also rather touching—the awkward effort of a huge corporation to demonstrate genuine caring. It even worked, a little. As part of a coordinated and coherent program, it might actually make me feel kindly toward a telephone company, which is no easy feat.

We also want more individualization in what we buy. We want it all to be as close to custom-made as possible. We want laundry soap that's perfect for a family whose children are grown. We want eight-course microwave meals for one. We want computers built to our personal specifications.

My mother lives in Florida now. She has a condo in that stretch of land that begins in Jacksonville and runs down the coast to Miami Beach with hardly a stop. I think there's a lot about the world I live in she wouldn't recognize or understand.

Our world is far more complicated and fragmented than hers was. We rarely have extended families anymore. The word *neighborhood*—or even *neighbor*—doesn't mean what it once did. I don't have any proof of this, but I think it's harder to make friends today than it once was. It's harder to connect and easier to be lonely in a crowd. And yet, we still feel the same human needs our parents did. Maybe we feel them even more acutely, since they're harder to fulfill.

It may be harder to make friends, but as far as brands go, we're being asked to make them faster than ever before. At the beginning of the twentieth century, it took brands a long time to reach the status of a household name. It could take a Kellogg's or a Campbell's twenty-five years or more to reach "superstar" brand status. Even twenty-five years ago, it took at least ten years for a brand to grow that large. But today, because of the media and communications outlets, a brand can grow almost overnight. That means brands are going to have to extend their virtual arms out to a lot of people in a short period of time to try and make them friends.

With the advent of the Internet, big companies aren't the only ones who can get the word out. Now every citizen with a computer can spread the word, good or bad, to millions of consumers around the world. Consumers have much more power than they ever had before.

If today's brands are to survive into the twenty-first century, they must be more customer oriented than ever before. A brand cannot grow without forming long-term relationships with each and every individual customer. Companies can no longer afford to hire brand managers who stick around for a year or two and then move on to the next project or product. Brand managers have to have long-term relationships with their brands, know the brand inside and out, understand its vision, and supervise its consistency.

The Four Necessities

Friendship Branding is a way that commercial entities can help people fill their friendship needs, even in today's world. What needs am I talking about here?

- *The need for human contact.* I don't want to count the hours I spend every week sitting in front of my computer screen, not seeing or talking to another human being. But I do know that every hour I spend this way adds to my sense of isolation. After a while, I yearn for human contact. Even a person's voice on the phone will do. But you can imagine how I feel when I get one of those computerized answering devices. They're always missing the option I want most: Press one if you hate talking to machines.

  An article entitled "The Store Is the Brand," by Janet Holt-Johnstone, in the 1998 issue of *Furniture World* magazine, stated: "Surveys indicate trips to shopping malls are down 35 percent and hours spent there 70 percent. People just don't have time anymore. So you must see to it that the trip is worthwhile and exciting for shoppers who visit your store . . . they must feel an affinity with you. If there's no relationship, you cannot create a branded future. . . . Customers talk about shopping as . . . something they enjoy. When stores let them down, they resent it in personal terms."

- *The need for community.* I like to belong. We all do. I need to feel a part of something—that I'm a member of many communities. I like being an American, a New Yorker, a woman, a bargain hunter, an East Sider, a *Times* reader, a frequent traveler, a *Today Show* watcher. I belong to all of these groups and many more. They help me to make sense of my life and to understand who I am. And they put me at least in emotional touch with others like myself. Belonging to a community helps me feel connected.

- *The need for trust.* In my parents' era, trusting wasn't the issue it is today. The world was smaller in many respects. We knew the shopkeeper, and he knew us. We knew the beat policeman. We trusted most people we met because we weren't often disappointed or lied to. But the world is much more impersonal today. If anything, our need to trust others is more acute than ever, but trust comes much harder. I want to trust. I want to feel that the people around me won't lie, cheat, or steal.

- *The need for recognition.* Yes, I want my privacy. I don't want strangers knowing the details of my financial and social life, or about my health. But that's balanced against my need to be recognized for who I am. I love it when I walk into a store and I'm greeted by name. I'm delighted when Amazon.com sends me an e-mail telling me my favorite author has a new book out. I'm pleased when my garage tells me it's time to change the oil or to get my car inspected. When people recognize who I am, or what I'm likely to need, or what I prefer, it makes me feel good. It makes me feel that I matter to the other person. I don't feel like a stranger anymore. I feel *recognized*.

Friendship Branding can't substitute for real friends. It can't equal the emotional satisfaction that comes from a heart-to-heart talk with someone you know and love, or a weekend with your family, or a card game with friends. Pleasures like these can't be replaced by any kind of marketing or branding activity.

But Friendship Branding can touch the same emotional chords. It can inspire trust, confidence, and even affection. It can stimulate the kind of lifelong customer loyalty that happens today only by luck or accident. It is a very powerful marketing concept.

Stand Out from the Crowd

Everyone has a favorite brand. Whether it's Hellmann's Mayonnaise, Skippy Peanut Butter, Saturn cars, Kellogg's Corn Flakes, Coke or Pepsi, Ivory Snow, Crest or Colgate toothpaste, Mobil, Sears, Smuckers—these companies and their products are part of the nation's collective memory. They have a special meaning for us. Somehow they're comforting. They remind us of home and of our childhoods. They're like old friends.

And there are new brands popping up every day. Take the ubiquitous "10-10" discount phone services that offer low-price long-distance service. The public is being bombarded by commercials, print ads, and direct mail for dozens of these companies. Will any one of these brands become the one that everyone remembers? Not likely.

That's because these companies are taking the same impersonal approach that the old established brands took in the '60s and '70s: Appeal to the mass market. Communicate to the largest number of people possible. Cater to the market and not the individual consumer. However, as we enter the new millennium, these kinds of brand communications—meant for everyone—make the product vulnerable to price. A competitor comes along and discounts the price and erodes any kind of brand loyalty that might exist.

Scott Bedbury, senior vice president of marketing at Starbucks Coffee Company told *Fast Company* magazine (August 1997) that a great brand is hard to find. "I walked through a hardware store last night and I came across fifty brands I didn't know existed," said Bedbury. "They may be great products, but they're not great brands."

That's because new brands cannot rely on old methods. Today, the consumer's battle cry is "Attention must be paid!" The value-conscious, discerning consumer is armed with all kinds of information he or she never had before. For example, he or she might know the actual cost of a car, or about available choices in utility companies, or about one-stop Internet price comparisons. The new, enlightened consumer has to be noticed, understood, and catered to. Even in high tech (or especially in the age of high tech), the new consumer wants to establish a personal relationship with a brand.

Take, for instance, a company like 1-800-FLOWERS, a large multi-million dollar company. This is a company that understands it takes more than a name to make a brand (see Figure 2.1). The letter they sent me last year addresses me by my first name. It acknowledges me as an important customer. And best of all, it includes an offer for a free bouquet from a store right in my neighborhood! It makes me feel as if company president Jim McCann himself appreciates and values the relationship I have formed with his company. Even though I know that thousands of other people received similar letters, it bonded me to the 1-800-FLOWERS brand. I felt as though I had found a friend.

It's the kind of personal touch that always gets me thinking about brands, about friendship, and about the relationship between the two.

But there are some companies that stand out from the crowd. Take Hallmark cards. When customers buy Hallmark cards, they really feel like they're buying the best. Watching the commercial in which a young student hides a greeting card behind her music for her "grouchy" piano teacher, viewers know that that little girl cares enough to send the very best—and the teacher really appreciates it. When Hallmark offers customers its Gold Crown program and gives them free merchandise and special offers after a certain number of purchases, it's employing Friendship Branding. Hallmark works hard at continuing the strong relationship and good feelings it expresses through its quality products and brand image.

What does Hallmark know that other companies do not? They know about Friendship Branding. This means creating brands that are more than logos and slogans, brands that are based on a customer's total shopping experience, brands that routinely provide distinctive customer satisfaction and often go above and beyond what is normally expected.

001542

Flowers mean the world to us.℠

December 1

Dear Lois,

I just wanted to personally thank you for choosing 1-800-FLOWERS this past year. I hope we made your celebrations in 1998 even more special.

To show our appreciation, there's a <u>free</u> "thank-you" bouquet waiting for you at our 1-800-FLOWERS store at 576 3rd Avenue at 38th Street in New York City. It's a special arrangement of colorful blooms and greens, wrapped and ready for you to drop into a vase. <u>To get yours, just come in by December 31, 1998 and show the florist this note</u>.

Here's our holiday catalog, too! Remember, any gift you choose comes fresh from our growers' farms around the world - the reddest reds, brightest yellows and the crispest, most fragrant evergreens on Earth.

So this year, ring in the holiday season with truly festive flowers. Come into one of our stores, click on www.1800flowers.com or call 1-800-FLOWERS (1-800-356-9377). And thanks again for your business!

Happy holidays,

Jim McCann

P.S. Enjoy the <u>free</u> bouquet of fresh flowers! You can pick it up at the 1-800-FLOWERS store in New York City. Just bring this note with you by December 31, 1998.

BC98-B

Figure 2.1 This personalized letter from 1-800-FLOWERS recognizes me as a valued customer with an offer for a free bouquet.

Jeff Bezos, founder and CEO of Amazon.com explains the concept well in a 1999 issue of the *Wall Street Journal*, "A brand is a relationship between you and your customer, and ultimately what's important is not what you send out to them in advertising, etc., but what they reflect back and how you respond to that."

That's not just talk from Amazon.com. If you order a book from Amazon.com online, you immediately get an e-mail confirmation of your order. The books arrive within two to three days. Then you get an e-mail thank-you note for your order. Not only that, but the next time you click on Amazon.com, they recommend similar books on the subject in case you might be interested in another purchase. Even though you know that this is a computerized service that Amazon.com provides for each one of its customers, it still makes you feel special and cared for.

Relationship Marketing

For years, marketers have been trying to figure out why people are loyal to some brands, products, or services, and not to others. One of the answers they came up with is that customers want to form relationships with the people they buy from—hence the frequently used industry buzz phrase "relationship marketing." The problem with that answer was that no one could define what that relationship is, how it is maintained (or lost), or how to make the most of it.

It turns out, though, that the answer is really simple. The relationship customers are striving for is friendship. Connection. The real reason people buy the same product over and over again, or are loyal to a particular company or service provider, is because they look upon that product or company as a true friend.

One clear example (among many) is the QVC shopping network. When the show host talks to callers over the phone, she calls them by name. She asks them about their lives, their families. If the viewer says she's buying a gift for her son, the host asks, "What's your son's name?" and then says something like "I know Johnny will enjoy his new camera, and he'll love you for getting it for him." Hosts talk about their own families, and viewers are often privy to the names, ages, and escapades of the host's children and spouses. And QVC has gone on the road, broadcasting live from each of the fifty states, the better to personally relate to their huge customer base.

A Friendship-Starved Nation

The reason this friendship relationship works is because, as a nation, we're friendship starved. We have busy lives. We're busy making a living, raising children. We have so many things on our plates that friendship sometimes gets the short shrift. So people call QVC and reach out to the show hosts and their guests to make friends. Customers read over their program guides to see when Joan Rivers will appear with favorite host Kathy Levin. Then they call in and greet them like long lost friends—"Hi Kathy. How are you tonight?" or "It's so great to speak to you, Joan." QVC operators are pleasant and helpful. Items are packaged carefully and sent with a clearly marked return label and policy that lets customers know they have thirty days to change their minds, no questions asked. This is one of the most blatant, and most effective, examples of Friendship Branding around today.

Friendship Branding works the other way too. We really take it personally when a brand lets us down. In October of 1999, Apple Computers announced that it was going to retroactively raise prices on some computers that customers had already ordered and paid for. The company had taken orders for a new, faster-than-ever computer but experienced delays in getting the necessary computer chips. When those customers tried to reorder the machines, they were charged $350 more than before.

According to an article on ABCNews.com, reported by David E. Kalish, this was a controversy that threatened Apple's public image. "This will probably go down in the record books as the most customer-unfriendly act this year, if not the last twenty years," said Rob Enderle, an analyst at the Giga Information Group, a consulting firm in San Jose, California. "It should be No. 1 on the list of how to send people to other companies."

Businesses are governed by the relationships they create and keep, and the impression they put out to their consumers. In today's world, a company needs to embrace the principles of friendship with conviction. Friendship Branding should encompass every aspect of how a company interacts with customers. So how exactly do you begin to develop a "friendly brand?" Let's take a look at the next chapter.

Chapter Summary

- If today's brands are to survive into the twenty-first century, they must be more customer oriented than ever before. A brand cannot grow without forming long-term relationships with each and every individual customer.

- Friendship Branding is a way that commercial entities can help people fill their friendship needs, even in today's world. It addresses four primary needs:

  1. The need for human contact
  2. The need for community
  3. The need for trust
  4. The need for recognition

- For a brand to succeed, it needs to distinguish itself from its competitors. This means creating a brand that is more than a logo and a slogan. A brand must be based on a customer's total shopping experience. A brand "that stands out" routinely provides distinctive customer satisfaction and often goes above and beyond what is normally expected.

- The reason people buy the same product over and over again, the reason people are loyal to a particular company or service provider, is because they look upon that product or company as a true friend. They "can count on" the company to deliver on its promise of a superior product, service, or exceptional value.

You just don't luck into things as much as you'd like to think you do. You build step by step, whether it's friendships or opportunities.

—*Barbara Bush*

Chapter Three

Developing a Brand in a World That Values Friendship

When clients come in to our agency to talk about their brand, we always begin by asking them about the essence of their company and what they are willing to do to get and keep customers. When they come back for the second meeting, they usually try to "show us" their brand, and they put their style manual on our conference table. It's usually a large loose-leaf binder. Then they show us their stationery and most recent advertising campaigns. They rarely talk about their customers— about how customers perceive them and how they work to communicate their image and personality to their target market.

Recently, a computer supply and accessory company came to Mason and Geller to develop a marketing campaign. I asked them if they had a brand personality. They patiently explained that because of the technical nature of their products, if they had a personality, they would not be perceived as a "serious" company.

But that's just not true. All you have to do is look at New Pig, a company that sells products to clean up industrial waste. They have become a leader in this field because of (1) the quality of their products and (2) the brand personality they developed. Their catalog stars a pig who appears on each page telling customers special benefits of the products. Fallacies about cleanup problems are highlighted in "Hog Wash" graphics. Their telephone number is 1-800-HOT HOGS. Most of all, however, they don't see their customers as "industrial plants" in need of cleanup. Their customers are the individuals within those plants, and their main concern is forming relationships with those people.

New Pig stepped out of the box and jumped way out in front of the competition.

And most companies can do the same, if they work step-by-step and become committed to the process of branding.

Basically, developing a brand involves looking at a company's past and present and then conceiving a cohesive personality for the companies and products going forward. Following are some ideas to get you on track.

Step 1: Background

This is a history of your company, or everything that has gotten you to this point. Background includes the following:

- How your company began and grew
- Physical description of the products(s) or service(s)

- Functions of these products or services
- Benefits (real or emotional) that these products or services fulfill for customers
- Unique properties of your products or services—that which makes them different from the competition
- Key factors that spurred the growth of your company
- Your key players now and your key players in the past
- Unique qualities of your company's corporate cultural
- Pricing
- Unique features of the physical location or environment of your company
- Line extension—present or future products that might be sold in conjunction or as an accessory to current ones

It is important that you think freely about your company and your business and come up with some of the unique characteristics that define "who you are."

Does your chairman or president have a distinct personality? For instance, Herb Kelleher at Southwest Airlines is a very humorous man, and this humor comes across in the branding of the company.

Maybe somewhere in the background, while they were working on their brand, Perdue talked about their founder, Frank Perdue, as a tough man—and then later on, their tagline for their brand became "It takes a tough man to make a tender chicken."

In the background, talk about the family who owns the business, how the product or service has changed over the years, the company culture, even the geographic features of the area in which the company resides. All of these items can be important.

Step 2: Competitive Analysis

Who are your competitors? Do they deliver a product or service that is different than yours? How is their product or service different than yours? Why would people prefer their company to yours? Do they provide greater value? Are their customers more loyal? Is their company growing faster than yours? Do they have better customer relationships? Why? You should list the companies that are your competitors—both in bricks and mortar, and on the Internet.

We had a vitamin company come into our agency that wanted to bring a "fat blocker" to market. They asked us to do a competitive analysis, and we discovered that there were several other companies offering lower price points and sometimes even a "free first month's supply." Our best strategy was not to compete on price but rather to offer more value. We decided to put a more human face on this brand and work to build relationships with customers. We put together a plan that included a spokesperson for the product and membership in an online community.

While you are looking at your competitors, keep an eye out for companies that might be branching out into your business and consider these as part of your competitive analysis.

Another way to find out about your competition is very simple: Buy something from each of your major competitors. Experience being their customer and then buy something from your own company (anonymously, of course).

Step 3: Positioning

How do you describe yourself in relation to your competitors? Carefully define who your target market is, and then think about "where you are" compared to your competitors. The way you position your company is the way you define your company so that prospects remember what's unique about you.

One of the best ways to accomplish this is to create a positioning map. Figure 3.1 represents a "positioning map" of several retailers and designers that offer women's clothing.

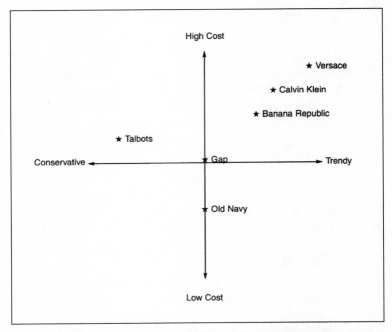

Figure 3.1 A positioning matrix helps to identify the perception of your product or service relative to your competitors.

For the purpose of this exercise, we compare the companies based on the relative cost of the clothes (low to high), as well as the relative "style" (conservative to trendy). The companies being considered here are Old Navy, Gap, Talbots, Banana Republic, Calvin Klein, and Versace.

Obviously this is not a science. To some extent, it's subjective and based on the individual's perceptions. In addition, companies frequently change their positioning. A few years ago, Talbots repositioned their clothes for a younger more fashionable consumer and sales fell dramatically. It seemed their efforts alienated their core customers. So they have "repositioned" their clothing line back to where it was originally.

Once you can visualize where you are in a positioning matrix, you can better see whether your area is crowded and then have an opportunity to change your business model and move to an area where there might be more opportunity for your company's product or services. *Positioning is finding a need in the marketplace that you are uniquely able to fill.*

Step 4: SWOT-F Analysis

Now that you've re-examined the history and background of your company, looked at the competition, and determined your unique positioning, a SWOT-F analysis allows you to begin charting a course for the future.

A SWOT-F analysis is best accomplished by putting together a group of people who really understand your company and people who work in various areas of it. I would include people in product development, marketing, customer service, and financial and let them go through the exercise of figuring out the strengths, weaknesses, opportunities, and "friendliness" of, as well as threats to, your company's brand.

- S—Strengths: What are the brand's "strong suits"?
  - Is there brand recognition?
  - How is the brand perceived by customers and prospects?
  - What is the key reason people like the brand?
  - If you're just launching your company, what do you anticipate the strengths of the brand will be?
  - What are the strengths for each product or service?

- W—Weaknesses: What are the problems with the brand?
  - Have you had a problem that wasn't handled well?
  - Is your brand perceived as too big and impersonal?
  - Have you been in business many, many years and stayed pretty much the same? Are you perceived as an old brand?

- O—Opportunities: What are the possibilities?
  - What unique strengths can you use to your advantage?
  - What important trends will benefit your products and company?
  - Where can you identify opportunities based on your customers' needs?

- Strategic programs
- Cross-marketing with partners

- T—Threats: What stands in the way of your brand?
  - Competition
  - Keeping up with the latest, newest, best products and services
  - Inability to continually meet customers' needs

- F—Friendship Quotient Analysis: Are you making your brand a "friendship brand"?
  - Is each and every customer contact positive for customers?
  - Are people on the front lines empowered to resolve any customer problem quickly—as a friend would?
  - Are your customers loyal? If customers aren't coming back, there must be a reason.
  - Are you treating your best customers really well?

Another way to assess your organization's strengths and weaknesses is by listening to your customers. Do you remember the person who wrote to you and told you he was having a love affair with your product or service? Well, review what he liked most about it. Also, spend even more time reviewing complaints or challenges. One way to do that is to listen in on customer service calls to get a sense of what are common issues among your customers and how well your customer service staff responds to these problems.

Now that you have all this information, here are some of the "next steps" you will want to take:

- Use the information to create a brand personality. Develop all your collateral materials and advertising with this personality in mind.
- If you have an agency, share this information with them. You'll want to incorporate this thinking into upcoming advertising and direct marketing campaigns.
- Think about ways to incorporate your brand's personality into communications with customers and prospects so that they will want to be your friends. Create a "brand voice book" based on your unique brand's personality. It will allow you to start thinking about how you want your company to "look" and "sound."
- Appoint someone to be the "Guardian of the Brand." This assures that there is monitoring and that the brand will be promoted correctly. Meet with the Guardian and other key players quarterly to review advertising as well as all the ways that the company interfaces with customers—be it Web sites, call centers, direct mail—and make sure that all is on track.

Competition is fierce. To survive and thrive, companies need to make themselves exceptional in the eyes of their customers. I believe that the way companies can do this is through Friendship Branding. In fact, it may be the only way.

People want to be treated well with every single contact they have with a company. They want to be treated as friends, and if they're not, they're going to defect.

Friendship Branding should be part of every single area of your company that touches the customer—e-commerce, advertising, public relations, direct marketing, customer service, retail outlets and catalogs—so that your customers' interactions with your company are always—*consistently*—good. Plain and simple—we do business with companies we like.

When every employee in your organization understands and buys into Friendship Branding, its power becomes even stronger. Their enthusiasm will spread to your customers and prospects. So begin today making your company a Friendship Brand.

Chapter Summary

- In order to become committed to the process of branding, companies must focus on customers' perceptions—how customers and the rest of the world perceive their products, services, and organization as a whole. The key issues are articulating and defining the brand and then determining how best to communicate this image and personality to the audience.

- Developing a brand is a process that begins with input about the company—its past, its founders, its products.

  - Background
  - Competitive analysis
  - Positioning

- SWOT-F
  - Strengths
  - Weaknesses
  - Opportunities
  - Threats
  - Friendship quotient
- Take action. Once you've done the work, put together a timeline that includes action steps and a date for the completion of each. That way your company will begin to become a Friendship Brand and be accountable in the near future.

There is a definite process by which one makes people into friends.

—*Rebecca West*

Chapter Four

The Eight Stages of Friendship Branding

Friendship Branding isn't a technique you can decide on today and implement tomorrow. It takes thought . . . and planning . . . and everyone in the company has to buy into it. I've divided the process into eight stages.

Stage One:
Putting a Human Face on Your Company

By their very nature, brands—especially large brands—are about as warm and human as a concrete block. And it's hard to feel friendly toward a concrete block. So it's important that you do everything you can to humanize your brand and your products or services. That means developing some human characteristics, such as humor, generosity, understanding, and helpfulness. Magazines like *Women's Day* and *Family Circle* are older brands that have moved with the times—while "staying true" to their "personalities." Buyers of these magazines can pick them up at supermarket checkouts as a treat—and read about 408 ways to wrap a present. These magazines make and stay friends with their readers.

Delias is an apparel company for preteen and teen girls. Through their catalog and Web site, they are creating a unique personality that reflects and attracts their target audience. Through the style of the catalog and site, as well as the copy, the Delias girl is fun loving, relaxed, and into cute stuff!

But remember, Friendship Branding is not about "talking the talk" but rather about "walking the walk." The essence of Friendship Branding is "action"—specifically, what you, as a company, are willing to do to keep customers happy.

Stage Two:
First Impressions for a Lasting Friendship

Before you can offer your friendship, you have to know who you are. You have to know what impression you're making. You have to have a unique and positive personality, something that comes from within, that goes deeper than shrink-wrap. Without that, you are just going through the motions. Here is a list of just some of the companies that have succeeded in creating brands that are defined, focused, and personable:

- Tiffany & Co.: While "Tiffany & Co." is the official name, "Tiffany's" is the company's familiar nickname.

Everything about Tiffany's says . . . well, "Tiffany's!" It's elegant; it's special. We like to have "classy" friends, and a gift from Tiffany's reflects well on the person who sends it.

- Fast Company: Whether or not the dot-com phenomena and culture is of interest to you, the magazine *Fast Company* has developed a relevant, irreverent, fast-forward persona.

- Burt's Bees: Who would have thought that some down-home, older than your average farmer-type guy would be credited with creating and bringing to market the lip balm that's on everyone's lips? And now there are even more Burt's Bees products flying off the shelves.

- Virgin Atlantic: That is one cool airline. It's something different, something really "one of a kind." And with individual movie screens, on-board manicures, and massages, they treat passengers as individuals.

It's important that you deliver on the first impression. If your customer's first impression of you truly reflects your company, then an implied promise is kept—you are what you say you are. Trust builds and a friendship can begin.

Stage Three:
How to Connect with the Right Customers

All of us have the ability to be friendly to practically everyone we meet. But genuine friendship comes from something deeper; it comes from common goals, common interests, common needs. In the same way, Friendship Branding must be aimed at the people who are in the right mindset, people who need it and will appreciate it.

We need to communicate our brand to the people who have the potential to feel passionately about us. People connect with brands and become involved with brands that they view as a reflection of the person they are or the person they aspire to become. *Martha Stewart Magazine* would be a great example of a brand that has a loyal, devoted following for this reason.

To attract people to your brand, your persona has to be clearly articulated in all media. If there are many different versions of your company being advertised—for instance, one image in print, another in radio—people will be confused. Again, Martha Stewart, as a brand, is a perfect example. In all variations—the books, the magazine, the television show, the catalog, the products—there is a consistent vision. Even the Martha Stewart line at Kmart, with its classic approach, fits into the brand.

Once you are certain you have a strong consistent brand persona, you can then begin to decide how to bring your company and product to the attention of your target market.

Stage Four:
Listening to Your Customers

According to practically every marriage book that's ever been written, when a marriage fails, it's usually a matter of poor communication. Someone has been a bad listener. It's the same with friendships. And it's the same with Friendship Branding. It's partly a matter of becoming the best listener you can be.

One way of "listening" to customers is to look at their behavior. As we all know, actions often speak louder than words.

All feedback, good or bad, is a tremendous opportunity. Usually, we don't hear why customers are unhappy; they just stop doing business with us. Thus, even negative feedback is an exceptional chance to make improvements.

There are many ways of getting to know customers. What's most important is the commitment at all levels to both resolve problems and address the underlying issues so that these situations don't happen again.

Stage Five:
Sharing with Your Customers

Of course, listening well is only one half of good communications. The other half lies in telling the other party in the relationship what he or she needs to know, in sharing crucial information, even some information that is traditionally confidential. Once we see the value of Friendship Branding, it's clear that we need to be willing to be more open about who we are as a company and about specific developments in our organization.

It's important that customers hear of any major developments from the company itself, not from an outside source. Nothing destroys trust faster than betrayal.

For instance, in 2000, Ford Motor Company clearly had a problem with their tires, which were alleged to be blowing out at high speeds. They handled this by implying that the problem was not theirs. Instead of taking responsibility, they tried to shift blame to Firestone, their supplier. This is a prime example of poor crisis management. They should have put customers first and contacted all owners of vehicles with the suspect tires immediately and offered to change them for no charge. The result of how they managed this situation is that Ford lost much of the respect, trust, and goodwill of their customers.

Instead of seeing customers as prey, companies who practice Friendship Branding see customers are "partners" who are entitled to know about certain aspects of a company.

Stage Six:
Making Customers Feel Secure

Above all else, customers must know they can *trust* your company, your product, and your service. They must feel that you will always be honorable in your dealings with them. Companies need to not only *act* trustworthy but also *be* trustworthy. They must take the high road with issues of privacy; they must describe their offerings clearly and honestly; they must provide customers with no-hassle returns and a full guarantee.

The object of Friendship Branding is to create an emotional bond—and the foundation of that bond is trust. Companies who treat their customers with compassion will stand out from the crowd. To accomplish this, companies need to teach their employees how to make customers feel as though they have a friend on their side—behind the counter or on the phone.

Stage Seven:
Building Trust Between You and Your Customers

This is about developing loyal customers. Like loyal friends, loyal customers are there for the long haul. They stay with you through thick and thin.

To have loyal customers, you must become a company that is worth being loyal to. Your commitment to customers must be unwavering. Customers must never feel neglected.

Also, companies must acknowledge loyal customers, make them feel special, and treat them well. They must get the same consideration you give really good friends.

Stage Eight:
Creating Friendships That Last

Trust is crucial, but it takes more than trust.

In an article in the *New York Times*, dated November 17, 2000, about branding and political parties, Patricia Winters Lauro explains: "Trust alone is not enough to keep a customer loyal. To keep customers, brands need also to establish other attributes like a 'care for me' relationship style that includes empathy and reciprocity."

In every interaction between the company and the potential customer (or the current customer), the behavior of the customer service rep or salesperson, the shipping, the packaging, the advertising, and the promotion is either supporting Friendship Branding or it's not.

And even when great care is taken, things don't always go as planned. What do friends do when something goes wrong? They make it right, of course. Usually, they can't rest until whatever went wrong has been completely repaired. That's part of Friendship Branding as well. And what do friends do when all is well? They make it even better. They exceed expectations. And so it is with Friendship Branding.

Laughter is not at all a bad beginning for a friendship, and it is far the best ending for one.

—*Voltaire*

Chapter Five

Stage One: Putting a Human Face on Your Company

The first rule of adding the human touch is to make sure your company shows your customers a human side, through humor, compassion, generosity, understanding, and helpfulness.

It seems like such an elementary concept—treating your customers like human beings. Yet there are many, many companies in existence today that do not take this concept to heart. They don't see individual buyers; they see dollar signs and profit margins. They will try anything they can think of— even if it is deceptive or misleading—to bring in more dollar signs and raise profit margins. These companies are not interested in building long-term relationships with anything but the almighty dollar.

But there are exceptions. For instance in speaking to Gun Denhart, founder and chairman of the Hanna Andersson mail-order catalog, she explains, "When I think of my customers, I think of them one at a time. It's not like I'm selling to a whole universe out there. The core of our business is that we treat each of our customers the way we want to be treated, like a human being."

There are other companies, however, like Hanna Andersson, that believe that the road to success is lined with the human touch. The more technologically sophisticated our world becomes, the more we crave human connection. Almost twenty years ago, John Naisbitt wrote in *Megatrends*, his seminal book: "The more technology around us, the more the need for human touch." And that was long before laptop computers, cell phones, the Internet, and e-mail.

But it was, coincidentally, around the same time that Gun Denhart and her husband, Tom, started their business in Portland, Oregon. Gun was searching for high-quality all-cotton clothes for her newborn son, clothes like the ones she had grown up with in Sweden. When she couldn't find them here in America, she and Tom decided to start the mail-order company, and to name it after her grandmother, Hanna Andersson. Since the beginning, the Denharts have been dedicated to keeping the human touch a strong part of their business, and that means treating customers like friends.

"When I look for a friend, I look for someone I can trust," says Gun. "And I think that our customers look for that in us. I want our customers to feel that they can trust what we say. That's why we're very particular that whatever we write is absolutely true and sincere" (see Figure 5.1).

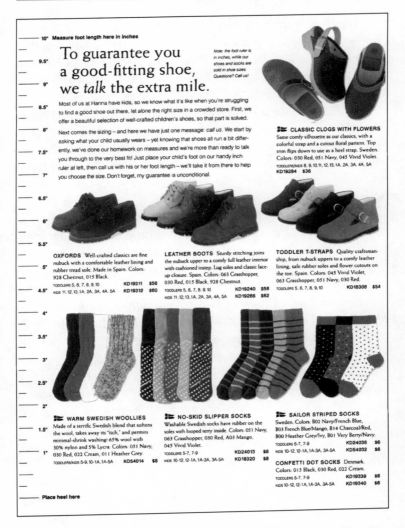

Figure 5.1 This catalog page from Hanna Andersson includes a handy ruler to help parents choose the right size footwear.

When a Hanna Andersson catalog says the clothes are comfortable, they mean it. The clothes are made so that "kids can be kids" in them. Parents constantly tell Gun that when given a choice, their children choose Hanna Andersson clothes to wear. One letter, of which Gun is especially proud, came straight from a seven-year-old, who wrote, "Dear Hanna Andersson, You are my favorite clothes store. I love your tights. Be happy, because I'm not usually interested in clothes. I also like your skirts, especially the black wool skirt. Maybe when I grow up, I will work for Hanna Andersson." High praise indeed!

But the one factor that makes Hanna Andersson stand out even amongst other "human" companies is its long-standing commitment to charity and community involvement. When the Denharts started their company, they realized that their clothes lasted for more than one child. So they began the Hannadowns Program, which encouraged customers to send used "Hannas" back to the company in return for a 20 percent credit toward their next purchase. The used clothing was then donated to children in need worldwide.

"We started the Hannadowns Programs our very first year," says Gun. "I have visited some of the Hannadowns recipients, mostly children of pregnant teenagers. I was just amazed that there were so many children in need. Twenty-five percent of children in America live below the poverty level. And even many of those who are above the poverty level still have very, very little."

The program has changed over the last few years. Although customers are no longer offered a credit, they are urged to donate their used "Hannas" to local charities, to the Massachusetts Coalition for the Homeless in Boston, or to the

Hamilton Family Center in San Francisco. And the Hannadowns Children's Fund distributes 5 percent of the company's pretax profits to charities working with children (Figure 5.2).

Although Hanna Andersson's customers initially choose this company for the quality clothing it offers, they remain loyal because of the personal touches in the catalog (e.g., stories of Gun's relatives and Swedish heritage), and because of the company's extraordinary commitment to the people they serve.

Connections Through Humor

While Hanna Andersson uses family and charity to give the company its human touch, many other companies rely on humor. Humor can work in many ways to strengthen the customer/company connection, just as it can be used to

Dear Friends,

The idea for Hannadowns' began with the realization that hannas last for more than one child. Rather than waste, why not pass clothes on to children in need? During Hanna's first fifteen years our customers have donated nearly one million pieces of recycled clothes to kids in need – and this is only the beginning!

We've now found two worthy charitable partners, one on each side of the country. If you don't already know of a local charity, please feel free to send your outgrown children's hannas to either *Massachusetts Coalition for the Homeless* in Boston or *Hamilton Family Center* in San Francisco (please see the order panel for address information). During recent visits to both, I was moved by the loving dedication and hard work of people who strive to make a real difference in the face of overwhelming need.

For more information about the Hannadowns Children's Fund and all the recipients of our 5% donation of pre-tax profits, visit our Web site Community Involvement pages. We hope to see you there!

hanna

P.S. Ideas? Write me via e-mail at hanna@hannaAndersson.com or, I'm usually taking calls Tuesdays 10am to 12pm PT.

Figure 5.2 Gun Denhart (alias Hanna) lets her customers know about the Hannadowns Children's Fund in her catalog; she also invites them to call or e-mail her personally.

strengthen the bonds of friendship. There is no one who can cheer up a person better than a friend. Everyone likes to be with people who have a sense of humor, people who can laugh at themselves (or at least don't take themselves too seriously) and can make us laugh, too.

Humor can be used to diffuse a serious situation or subject. Until recently, there were certain industries, such as banking and insurance, that would never have used humor in their marketing or advertising. But a few years ago, Metropolitan Life Insurance (now known as MetLife) broke that mold by licensing Charles Schultz's Peanuts characters to represent the company. These characters come with a well-known, gentle type of humor that make the serious subject of insurance more approachable and less daunting to the average consumer. If an insurance agent comes to you "introduced" by Snoopy or Charlie Brown, it's much easier to see her (and the company she represents) as a friend.

Insurance is still a serious business, and these cartoon characters don't negate that. But MetLife has been able to use them to lighten up the heavy responsibility of one of life's necessary and not always pleasant tasks—that is, buying insurance to protect ourselves, our families, and our property. The humor is used in a subtle, lighthearted manner.

It's not just large companies that can use the lighthearted touch to help customers feel connected. When Price Automotive, a Delaware car dealership, wanted to bring customers back to their service center, they were looking for a way to re-create relationships with both active and inactive customers. Car buyers usually stop using the dealership for service after their warranty runs out, and Price wanted to keep that relationship going.

So the creative team at Mason & Geller came up with the idea of "spokeswrenches"—two talking wrenches that talk directly to a customer in a personalized mailing (see Figure 5.3). Having your car serviced can be a great inconvenience to some people, so adding this humorous touch makes it seem like less of a big deal. It's a subtle message that says, "Not only are the people at Price Automotive friendly, their *tools* are friendly, too!"

One company that uses a broader approach to humor is Taco Bell. Today, Taco Bell is the nation's leading Mexican-style quick-service restaurant with over $5 billion in system-wide sales. There are more than 7,000 restaurants nationwide that serve more than 55 million customers each week.

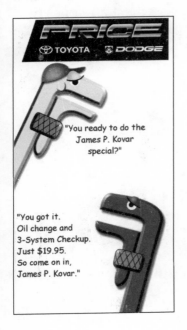

Figure 5.3   Creating these "spokes-wrenches" was a very effective way of giving Price Automotive person-ality while speaking directly to the customer.

Just a few years ago, Taco Bell was part of a fast-growing crowd of fast-food chains. Most of its advertising centered around pricing and specialty meal offers.

Then came . . . the Chihuahua (see Figure 5.4). From the minute that little dog with the big eyes appeared on the television screen, Taco Bell, and the catch phrase "Yo Quiero Taco Bell," became part of America's vernacular.

A 1997 press release from Taco Bell quoted Chuck Bennett, cocreative director of TBWA Chiat/Day, creators of the campaign, as saying: "We wanted the Chihuahua's character to be perceived as a 19-year-old guy in a dog's body who primarily thinks about food and girls." Ironically, the dog gave the company a human feel. That characterization came across clearly to consumers and gave them a fun new way to relate to the company. It also gave Taco Bell a distinctive personality.

Figure 5.4
The Taco Bell Chihauhua has become a national figure and has helped the brand stand out in the crowd of fast-food restaurants.

Who Speaks for You?

Humor, of course, does not just come from cartoon characters, dogs, and pigs. People can be funny too. Which brings us to the second rule of adding the human touch:

Put your people out front to humanize your company and give it an identity customers can understand, relate to, and be comfortable with.

Many companies hire spokespeople to "front" for their companies. These spokespeople can be celebrities (e.g., Michael Jordan for Nike, Cybill Shepherd for L'Oréal, and Candice Bergen for Sprint). Using celebrities can be very effective, but it can also be tricky. People tend to remember the celebrity but forget which product they're hawking. You've most likely had this conversation:

"Oh, I love that new commercial with Michael Jordan and the cartoon characters. You know the one I mean, with the bird and the cat . . . Oh, what's it for again? I can't remember what it's for, but I love the commercial."

Using celebrity endorsers can be dangerous. Remember Michael Jackson's short-lived commercials for Pepsi Cola? And what about Hertz Rent-a-Car and O. J. Simpson? Intellectually, everyone understands that the company is not responsible for the actions of its endorsers, but emotionally consumers can't help making an unfavorable connection.

A few years ago, I worked on a campaign for a diet program. We hired a celebrity spokesperson to use the product and lose weight. The campaign worked very well until six months later, when the celebrity put back all the weight he'd lost—and more. It didn't matter that he was no longer appearing as a spokesperson for the company; he was still a celebrity and was a constant visual reminder that our product did not necessarily produce long-lasting results.

Sometimes the best spokesperson of all is someone who is directly related to your company. After all, anyone can hire a spokesperson to represent them, if their pockets are deep enough. But someone who actually works at the company or, more often, owns the company, adds real credibility. Michael Eisner, chairman and CEO of the Walt Disney Company, is an example of someone who represents his company effectively. Millions of children (and their parents) watch him every Sunday on television as he introduces a Disney movie or special event. And he is someone who is willing to take a stand for the values of his company.

When Disney began running cruise ships, Eisner was encouraged to open casinos on the ships, because they are an important source of revenue. But Eisner refused, saying that Disney is a family company and that every Disney destination should be fun for the entire family. As a result, customers can relate to Eisner and his company as if they were friends next door. Parents can drop the kids off and not have to worry about them playing violent video games and watching X-rated movies.

Eisner is, of course, not the only company head who acts as a spokesperson for his company. What do these names bring to mind?—Michael Dell, Bill Gates, Lee Iacocca, Tom Carvel, Dave Thomas, and Frank Perdue. These are people we can relate to, perhaps as individuals we admire from afar as savvy businesspersons, or as individuals we relate to on a more intimate level as down-to-earth "men of the people."

One of the most famous of these front men is Herb Kelleher, chairman, president, and CEO of Southwest Airlines.

The company started in 1971 with a net loss of $3,753,000. The 1998 annual report celebrates the company's twenty-sixth year of profitability, with earnings of $433.4 million. The success of this no-frills, low-fare, no-food, no-assigned-seats airline is largely attributed to its attitude, fostered by Kelleher himself. It's an attitude that has led to such antics as flight attendants who sing safety instructions, and contests to see how many passengers can fit into the plane's rest room. Even the company's advertising carries through the "humor" theme (see Figure 5.5). Kelleher himself has been known to dress up like Elvis, belt out a rap song, and settle a dispute by arm wrestling.

Figure 5.5   Southwest Airlines President Herb Kelleher shows off his sense of humor in this "Born to Ship" ad for the airline's cargo service.

People love to fly Southwest Airlines. In a December 1998 article in *U.S. News & World Report,* Kelleher told reporter Katherine T. Beddingfield that fun is important because "people look for psychic satisfaction in everything they do. So if you have a flight where people enjoy themselves they may come back more often." People do come back often, because they enjoy the entire experience. They are treated like friends—friends who are on a budget. They are not wined and dined. But they are entertained. It's easy for Southwest customers to feel that they have a strong personal relationship with the Airline, its employees, and its CEO.

Recognize Your Employees

Every employee at Southwest Airlines is trained in their Friendship Branding philosophy, and every employee has the ability to break the rules to help a customer. It's the company's philosophy that customers are won or lost on the front lines, at the gates, or in flight. So the people who are in those positions have to be totally customer oriented.

In order to ensure that Southwest continues to attract high-caliber employees, it has started a program for elementary school children in fifty-two cities across the country. The Adopt-A-Pilot program teams a Southwest Airlines pilot with each of fifty-two classrooms. The pilots serve as adult mentors for the students in addition to providing the focal point of the program. Using official route maps, each class will follow its adopted pilot over the course of the four-week program. The classroom curriculum includes such subjects as math, geography, aviation principles, civics, writing, and research skills.

"As we continue to grow and implement new technology, we find ourselves in need of a more experienced, more sophisticated Employee," said Libby Sartain, Southwest's vice president of People (or human resources). "Our schools can't do it alone. We see the need, as a company, to be involved in education in order to increase the caliber of potential Employees for Southwest Airlines."

It is not often that companies empower their customer contact employees and teach them to be advocates or case-workers for their customers. A study conducted by UCLA on the reasons why customers leave or stop buying from a company showed that 1 percent leave because they die, 3 percent leave because they move, 5 percent leave because of word of mouth, 9 percent leave because of a change in quality of the product or service, 14 percent leave because of a change in price—and *68 percent* leave because of "an indifferent employee." That means that a vast majority of people stop buying from a particular company because of an unpleasant experience they had dealing with an employee.

Since not many customers get to deal with top management, those unpleasant experiences are occurring with sales clerks, cashiers, telemarketers, in-house operators, and customer service people. Yet, these are the people who consistently receive the least amount of training during the course of their employment. This does not make economic sense.

Customers now have more choices than ever before when they decide where to buy. If they so choose, they can go to the Internet and buy without having any human interaction at all. And yet, even when they choose the Internet, they want the simulated human contact of a "thank you" for their order, and an e-mail address so that they know any post-sale questions will be answered.

One of the biggest complaints that consumers have about customer contact people is that the contact people have no authority. It is not customary, for example, for operators to give out information or for cashiers to give refunds without consulting managers. I recently had some medical bills that were rejected by my HMO. I called several times to ask what the problem was. Each time I was told that I needed different information from my doctor. Not only was it inconvenient for me to make these calls, but also it was added work for my doctor's office. Even when I got the information, the HMO operators were not able to tell me whether I would be receiving a reimbursement check. At the end of this mess, I felt that they were giving me as hard a time as possible so that I would get frustrated and give up trying.

I did get frustrated—so frustrated, in fact, that I started exploring other options, and soon changed my medical coverage. Because of that treatment over a few hundred dollars, they lost my business altogether. And, since I run a business, they lost all of my employees' business as well.

One Australian company found out the importance of empowering employees the hard way. When the Spotlight company, Australia's largest chain of fabric, craft, and home interior stores, grew from one store to ten, its owners decided that a new management style was necessary. They hired a general manager to restructure the company. He created a detailed and highly regimented corporate hierarchy.

The company, which was family owned and run, had always had a relaxed, friendly atmosphere. Now, staff members had strict controls on how much stock they could order, and strict lines of communication to order more. When a customer came in and wanted, say, 20 yards of a certain material and there was only 10 yards in stock, the manager had to cut through miles of red tape just to get more. By that time, the customer had gone somewhere else.

Soon, management realized they were losing both employees and customers. So they restructured again, this time with the basic premise that the customer was the boss. The staff was retrained to use their own initiative and take much more responsibility.

As Ari Unglik wrote in *From Market to Marketing: The Spotlight Story:* "There is only one rule enforced at Spotlight—use your own best judgment at all times. . . . At the store level, if a customer wants a refund, the sales person needn't run to the manager, but simply use their best judgment—given their knowledge about the customer and the complaint—to make a decision. Mistakes are treated as learning experiences."

The only way that this system really works is if you put your faith and trust (and training) into your employees. This is part of what makes companies like Southwest, Dell, and Spotlight so successful. It's also part of the corporate culture at New Pig: "We believe that customers look for the same qualities in the companies they deal with as they look for when making a friend," says Doug Hershey. "They want someone who is easy to talk to. So we make it easy for our customers to talk to our people. I know many businesses that measure the amount of time an inbound operator spends on the phone, because they want it to be as short as possible. We don't do that. We encourage our people to develop relationships. So we tell them, if a guy is short and sweet and he wants to get off the phone, get him off. But if he's personable and wants to talk, go ahead and chat.

"The other thing customers look for is trust. Do I trust my friends? Yes, I do. So customers have to trust that New Pig will fulfill their orders, give them a quality product and a good value. And we've empowered our people on the phone so that they don't lose the trust of our customers. Just last week we had an inbound rep who took back $3,000 worth of product. It was his decision. He made the call, and we stick by it."

The Hanna Andersson company shares this philosophy. "Everything that touches the customer should be in the spirit of treating your customers like human beings," says Gun Denhart. "In terms of executing that, you have to treat your employees with the same warmth and respect you want them to have for customers. We keep everybody posted every month about how we're doing financially and about things that are going on, so that they can understand not just their part, but the overall picture. If you let them know that they are valued and that they are contributing to the overall scheme, then they can treat the customers in the same way."

It's in that spirit that the company participates in the Cash for Kids program. At the beginning of each school year, every school-age child of a Hanna Andersson employee receives a check for $100 to be used for something in his or her classroom. The kids and teachers decide together how to use the money.

"Locally, we've had a lot of problems with school budget cuts," says Denhart. "We're sending a message to the children that their education is not important. And that's not true. These kids feel so proud when they come in with the $100 check and they have a say in where the money goes. Even though it's a not a lot of money, the kids really feel empowered. And the employees really appreciate how it makes their kids feel."

Recognize Your Customers

You will find loyal employees at all of these companies not just because they are empowered but because they are recognized. Recognition is one of the greatest motivating factors for human beings. Customers, too, want to be recognized. They have needs, desires, hopes, and fears. They want these feelings to be acknowledged in some way; they want companies to show them they're not just names on an electronic file. That means calling them by name, always knowing the details of your relationship with them in the past (past purchases, returns, buying patterns, etc.)—in other words, by recognizing them whenever they show up.

One company that does an extraordinary job of recognizing their customers is Saturn. Saturn is a different kind of company that has convinced many people that it is a different kind of car. In fact, Saturns are not all that unique in their design or performance. But people have become friends with the brand.

Saturn was the first car company to introduce the "no hassle" buying policy, but that's only one of the reasons customers enjoy being Saturn owners. Saturn's customers are not only recognized as friends; they're also recognized as family. Once you become part of the Saturn family, you're invited to all kinds of special events, reunions, and parties. You can tour the factory and see exactly how "your" car is made. Saturn commercials feature employees and real-life customers who talk about what a wonderful experience it is to be part of the Saturn Friendship Branding experience.

Keep a Database

One of the reasons people treasure their friends is because they know one another so well. They share a history. Their friends know their taste, and what they like and dislike. They know the kinds of things they've done in the past and the kinds of things they're likely to do. They remember things that they find important, like how many years they've known each other, as well as purchases they've made together. Companies have the ability to know their customers almost as well. Advances in database technology now make it possible to collect and store a personal history of their relationship with each and every customer they have. They should know their taste, keep track of how long each person has been a customer, and know what they've purchased over the years.

All it takes to recognize customers is a database. Direct marketing has been using the database and the information it provides since the turn of the century (the last century, that is). Your database is your list of customers who have bought from you (or made inquiries about your products or services) before. A database tells you who has been a long-term customer, and who has just started buying from you. It also tells you who has defected and isn't buying from you anymore.

The most important information you can get from your database is determined by these three factors: recency, frequency, and monetary, or RFM.

Recency answers the question, When was the last time this customer ordered from you? This is a major factor; research tells us that customers who have recently bought from you have a high propensity to buy from you again. This is true in every industry (except real estate). It even works when customers buy automobiles. As soon as one family member gets a new car, another family member decides he or she has to have one too. You want to know who your most recent buyers are so that you can make them special offers.

Frequency refers to the number of times this customer has ordered from you.

Monetary refers to the average dollar amount of an order from that customer. (If the customer has made three purchases during the past year, one for $20, one for $105, and one for $40, then the average amount of her order for the year would be $55.)

One of the truest maxims of marketing is that it costs a lot more money to get a new customer than to keep the ones you have. So it makes economic sense to spend money on nurturing relationships with our best customers. That means recognizing, and rewarding, your best customers.

There are many ways of doing this, including special discounts, newsletters, exclusive merchandise, thank-you notes, and holiday and birthday greetings.

Birthdays are an effective way to recognize customers. Everyone feels that his or her birthday is special and looks forward to getting cards, calls, and e-mail greetings. Loehmann's, an off-price discount store, goes one step farther. Loehmann's card customers are invited to take 15 percent off all purchases on their birthday. My daughter-in-law plans her birthday celebrations around her visits to Loehmann's, and she hasn't missed one in years.

Everyone Can Add the Human Touch

As mentioned previously, New Pig does an exemplary job at "adding the human touch." In 1985, Don Beaver and Ben Stapelfeld were looking for a new approach to cleaning up oil and grease spills. The area the duo used for their experimentation became so messy that it soon became known as "the pig pen." They named the product that came out of that research the Pig® Absorbent Sock. From those humble beginnings, New Pig Corporation was born.

I was speaking with Doug Hershey, the company's executive vice president and he explained, "When we started in 1985, one of the things we did was look at other catalogs and advertisements in our industry, and they were boring and drab. So we said, 'Why can't we have fun?' Why can't it be a pleasurable experience for purchasing people and maintenance guys and safety engineers and plant managers to enjoy the ordering process? We wanted to differentiate ourselves, to have some fun, and we wanted to build relationships."

New Pig has been successful at all three of those goals. Over the years, they have expanded the Pig theme and set themselves apart from others in their field. *Management Review* magazine (January 1999) stated: "Branding the previously unbrandable has given the company a competitive advantage." Their Pigalog catalog (as their mail-order catalog is called) features pig cartoons throughout (see Figures 5.6 and 5.7); their address is One Pork Avenue.

Using humor is not all fun and games, however. You have to be careful that the humor doesn't go over the line. After all, you like your friends to be amusing, not obnoxious.

One slogan the company tried, "More suck for your buck," offended some customers. And one of the Pigalog catalog covers caused considerable controversy. "We had a lot of competitors coming out saying that their products were as good as ours," says Hershey. "So we designed a cover with one of our employees dressed as Elvis and a caption that said, 'Don't trust your leaks and spills to any imposter.' We got a lot of calls about that one. People thought we were being irreverent towards Elvis."

It's not only humor that New Pig passes along to its customers, though. The Pigalog catalog is filled not just with products; it's also filled with educational articles on such subjects as new environmental regulations and factory maintenance. This helps customers relate even more strongly to the company and lets them know that New Pig's first concern is helping customers "in relentless pursuit of clean."

Friendship Branding Works for All Companies, Big or Small

If you look at the companies studied in this chapter—companies like Hanna Andersson, New Pig, Saturn, Price Automotive, MetLife, Taco Bell, Southwest Airlines—you'll notice that they're all experts in adding the human touch. But they're not all the same size; they run the gamut from small to humongous. Friendship Branding is a great equalizer in that respect; any size company can use it effectively.

Figure 5.6 A flying pig graces this Pigalog catalog cover and promises customers fast delivery. The pig theme ironically adds a "human" touch to a company that deals with industrial waste.

Figure 5.7   The pig theme is carried throughout the catalog, making even a drum pallet seem like a fun item.

It's especially important, however, for large companies to keep the human touch in mind. And it's something that many large companies forget.

One large company that practices outstanding Friendship Branding is Home Depot, the world's largest home improvement retailer (in 1999, the company employed over 190,000 people). This is a company that definitely keeps the customer in mind. The salespeople know what they're talking about. There are plumbing specialists in the plumbing department, paint specialists in the paint department, and plant specialists in the garden centers. Every store offers free design and decorating consultations. And there are free in-store clinics to help homeowners develop their do-it-yourself skills.

Salespeople have been hired to be helpful and friendly. When I went shopping at Home Depot recently, I was apparently looking lost in the light bulb department. A salesperson came over and asked if I needed help. I told him that the regular bulbs in my home were not bright enough for reading. The man took me over to a section of round bulbs unlike any I had seen before. He explained how they were different from other bulbs and that they would fit into standard sockets. He spent more than fifteen minutes with me for a $30 purchase. At that moment, he and I, and Home Depot, had formed a perfect friendship.

So it's not the size of the company that counts; it's the attitude. Large companies often get into "unfriendly" branding when they see themselves, or their customers see them, as *institutions*. Telephone companies, utilities, credit card companies, and banks often fit into this category.

People don't trust institutions, and with good reason. It's because institutions don't think of their customers as human beings. Take phone companies, for instance. There is no real difference in the service you get from one phone company to another. You dial a number, you get someone on the line, you talk. In most cases, if you're calling from anywhere other than your own residence, you have no idea which phone company you're using.

So the only offer phone companies have is price. But even those offers are confusing, and somewhat deceptive. They keep lowering the cost-per-minute offers at the same time they raise the monthly fees (which they only tell you in the smallest of print on the last page of your phone bill). There is very little incentive for a customer to remain loyal to any one of these companies.

Credit card companies, too, have the institutional attitude. They're interested in luring in customers by offering low, low introductory rates—and then they make it very difficult to determine what your rate will be when the introductory rate expires.

The ultimate in institutional thinking, however, was demonstrated by one of the nation's largest banks when they tested a new program in my neighborhood. It was a new type of smart card. Unlike a debit card (which takes money out of your checking account when you pay for purchases), you actually loaded money (through your ATM) onto the card. So you could have a card worth $20, $200, or however much you chose to load onto the card. Then, when you went to a merchant who accepted this card, you could pay for items without using cash.

The problem with the card was that if it was lost, so was the money you had loaded onto it. No signature or pin number was required to use it, so anyone who picked it up could just spend your money! The only benefit that the bank offered in its promotion of this card was that it saved you the time of having to get correct change out of your pocket. Thinking there must be another benefit, I asked someone at the bank about it. He admitted to me that the major benefit was that this card was easier for the bank! This is not only institutional thinking; it is also extreme arrogance to put out a product that has no benefit except to your company. Needless to say, this card was a failure and was soon withdrawn from the market.

One of the problems is that institutions serve so many different people. Banks, utilities, and phone companies—and large companies in general—often have extensive product lines serving widely different clienteles. And they tend to say the same thing, to convey the same message, to all of those people. Their challenge is not just to say, "We're so large we can be everywhere and serve everybody," but to say, "We have the size and the expertise to handle your individual needs."

Jeff Bezos, founder of Amazon.com, was asked in a television interview if he could foresee a way that his company could fail. "The only way that we could fail is if we stop being obsessed with the customer," said Bezos. It's that obsession that ensures a company will add the human touch and engage in true Friendship Branding.

Chapter Summary

- Make sure your company shows its customers a human side, through humor, compassion, generosity, understanding, and helpfulness.

- Any brand can add a human touch—even if you're dealing with unusual products (such as those in the "relentless pursuit of clean").

- Put your people out front so that you can humanize your company and give it an identity customers can understand, relate to, and be comfortable with.

- Empower your employees so that they can make meaningful decisions on a one-to-one basis with customers.

- Recognize your customers through your database. Prioritize your customers using recency, frequency, and monetary.

- Remember that the best way for your brand to fail is to stop being obsessed with your customer.

Beautiful and rich is an old friendship,
Grateful to the touch as ancient ivory,
Smooth as aged wine, or sheen of tapestry
Where light has lingered, intimate and long.

Full of tears and warm is an old friendship
That asks no longer deeds of gallantry,
Or any deed at all—save that the friend shall be
Alive and breathing somewhere, like a song.

—Eunice Tietjens

Chapter Six

Stage Two: First Impressions for a Lasting Friendship

A few years ago, some friends and I went to a famous and popular New York City restaurant for a Valentine's Day brunch. Although I had heard many good things about the restaurant, I had never been there, and I didn't know what to expect.

Our group decided to go to this particular restaurant because of a well-placed, beautifully designed ad we saw in the newspaper promising a fun brunch and a pleasant atmosphere. When we arrived, we were greeted graciously, and each woman was handed one long-stemmed red rose and a box of Cracker Jacks, along with the assurance that the surprise in one lucky person's box would be a genuine diamond ring.

That imaginative touch was followed by a delicious meal, excellent service, and idyllic ambiance. My friends and I spent a delightful afternoon, and all agreed we would not only frequent this restaurant again but also recommend it to others (even though each of us dutifully ate our boxes of caramel corn without finding a diamond).

We chose the restaurant (1) because we had all heard of its excellent reputation and (2) because of the tantalizing ad we saw in the paper. Each of these factors made a favorable impression, which was delightfully reinforced by our brunch.

The restaurant was practicing Friendship Branding by delivering on its promise of a fun romantic way to spend Valentine's Day.

A Good First Impression Is Like a Promise Made

If your customer's first impression of you truly reflects your company, then a promise is kept, and a friendship is born. If the impression is false or misleading, a promise is broken, and the potential for friendship disappears.

Impressions can be made in a variety of ways. Let's face it, we're a judgmental society. We judge others by their appearance, their weight, their posture, their personality, their voice, their vocabulary. We judge them by the jobs they hold, by the hobbies they pursue, and by the people with whom they associate.

We also judge the people we meet on compatibility factors. Are they dressed in a style we admire or aspire to? Is their taste similar to our own? Do they have the same sense of humor or a similar seriousness of purpose?

We look for a certain consistency of character. If we meet them at a lively evening soiree, can we trust that they'll be just as interesting in the light of day? Will they say something one day, then turn around and say the opposite the next? Will they say one thing and do something else?

These factors help us form impressions of the people we meet. Some qualities might outshine others or be more prominent at first glance. But they are the qualities that can either attract people and make them want to get to know us better or turn people away without giving us a chance.

So we try to look nice, to put our best foot forward, when we're meeting someone new. We try to be friendly and to express interest in the details of our new acquaintance's life. This is a period of discovery, a time when two people are looking for information from each other. If the information is favorable on both sides, a relationship is formed. This is a ritual of courtship; it could turn into a one-night stand, lead to friendship (either short or long term), or even lead to marriage. That same relationship-building exercise happens when we are considering trying a new store, product, or service.

Nine Ways to Make a First Impression

1. Word of Mouth
Word of mouth has built many a faltering brand, and it has killed some as well. We tend to trust what our friends have to say, and if they tell us something is not good, we won't even try it. If, however, they heap praise on a product or brand, we want to see for ourselves.

The first time I ever heard of Dr. Pepper, I was passing through the small town of Coldwater, Michigan. A friend and I stopped into the grocery store on Main Street to get drinks for the car ride.

"Oh," she cried out, "they have Dr. Pepper!"

"Dr. What?" I asked.

"Dr. Pepper. It's this great soft drink they have down South. You've got to try it."

I did, I loved it, and I've been a Pepper fan ever since.

That was a memorable first encounter. But I could just as easily have been introduced to that brand in a number of different ways. If they were not as memorable, I might never have tried Dr. Pepper, much less become a loyal customer. There are nine important ways a brand can make a first impression, and you never know which one will be a customer's "first time." That's why every point of contact a customer *might* have with your product must be treated like the first and most important one that customer will ever make.

If my friend hadn't been so enthusiastic in her recommendation, I might have chosen another drink. But because she was actually excited to find this brand (at the time, it had limited regional distribution), she convinced me to try it as well. This type of first impression has the most impact. And yet, you don't know what a customer is going to say about your brand. The only thing you can do is make sure that every aspect of your brand lives up to the promise it makes; make sure it does what you say it will do, that it maintains a high degree of quality, and that it cares about what people have to say about it.

2. Advertising

Advertising involves paying the media (newspapers, magazines, radio, television, or the Internet) to place messages that position a product or company and build an image in customers' minds. With most major brands, advertising is the first impression the majority of potential customers get of a product or company, because advertising reaches the greatest number of people. It is usually the first thing that people notice about your brand. It allows potential customers to form a basic impression of who you are and what you are about. An Absolut vodka ad, for instance, tells consumers that this is a brand that is sophisticated, witty, even a little on the snobby side. An ad for Johnson's Baby Shampoo tells consumers the brand is loving, caring, and wholesome. The image has been planted, but it has yet to be confirmed. It's as if you see a stranger across a crowded room, get a feeling for the type of person he or she might be, but have not yet been introduced.

Advertising makes the shallowest impression, because you don't get to go into much detail in a television, radio, or print advertisement. So the impression has to be brief, strong, and clear. It also has to be placed in the proper context to reach the target audience. If it is not in the proper context, it will either be ignored or rejected.

It would be a perfect consumers' world if we could all make our buying decisions based on word of mouth. We would like someone we trust to give us a recommendation. But when that's not possible, the next best thing is that we trust the carrier of the advertising message. So, in addition to the ad itself, the consumer also judges a product according to what it's associated with. For instance, I watch the Lifetime channel ("television for women") on TV. If I see a product advertised there, I am likely to pay attention. It is as if I were being introduced to it by a friend. If I saw the same ad on a sports channel (which I don't usually watch), I probably wouldn't give it a second thought. It doesn't have the same impact, because I have no previous relationship with the sports channel.

3. Promotion

Promotion occurs when a company devises unusual ways to get customers to buy its products or services. Promotions can include free samples, coupons, discount offers, special sales, contests, sweepstakes, in-store celebrity appearances—anything that is used to encourage a purchase. A few years ago, there was a print ad for Absolut Citrus that featured a lemon rind encasing the familiar clear bottle. As an in-store promotion, the company produced three-dimensional versions of the ad, with a larger-than-life bottle and a bright yellow lemon rind that mechanically circled the bottle over and over again. It was quite striking, and effective. It was an extension of the brand's advertising, and for people coming in to buy liquor it was like running into an old friend in the store.

Promotions must be honest and straightforward to be effective. There should be no catch or fine print to make buyers feel manipulated. Last year, I took my mother shopping at a large department store in Florida. She was shopping for summer blouses. She is ninety years old, is difficult to fit, uses a cane, and doesn't shop that often. So we were quite pleased to see signs saying that certain famous maker blouses were on sale—"Buy two, get one free." We spent quite a long time choosing three blouses and trying them on.

When we got to the cashier, I was charged for all three. When I told the cashier that these were a "buy two, get one free" special, she said, "Oh no. What you have to do is buy two blouses, fill out this form, and send the form and the receipt to the company. Then they'll send you a free blouse." When I checked the signs again, I saw that this was explained in tiny, tiny print on the large signs. I felt cheated and manipulated. And to add insult to injury, when I helped my mother fill out the form to get the "free" blouse, I realized that the company would send her a blouse in her size—but they would choose the color, and she would have to pay a $3.95 shipping charge!

Needless to say, this was not an exercise in Friendship Branding. It was the company's way of getting rid of an overstock of blouses in unpopular colors. Neither my mother nor I will ever buy that brand again. And because of guilt by association, that department store has lost its trustworthiness in my eyes as well.

4. Public Relations

Simply put, public relations is free advertising (except for the fees you might pay to a public relations firm for getting your story in the press). It is exposure for the brand that is not paid for. It could be a feature article in a newspaper, appearances on radio or television talk shows, or opportunities for chatting live on the Internet.

Here is a perfect example of public relations: In 1984, I was working on a campaign to sell commemorative Olympic coins. We were using both advertising and direct mail to sell the coins. And the public relations department arranged for one of our coins to be tossed at that year's Super Bowl. We would never have been able to afford to buy advertising time in that slot; it's the most expensive television time of the year. But with no cost to us, the toss was seen by millions of TV viewers, and it helped sell hundreds of thousands of coins.

Public relations is frequently an effective Friendship Branding tool because it brings consumers closer to the brand. It allows us to get to know the brand and/or the people behind it.

For instance, a television program recently profiled Marvin Eisenstadt, owner of the company that makes Sweet 'N Low sugar substitute. This is not a company that's often in the news. The program mentioned that when Eisenstadt retooled his factory recently, he made certain that not one of his employees would lose his or her job due to modernization of the plant. During that modernization, Eisenstadt added a machine that automatically counts out 100 packets of Sweet 'N Low in boxes. But at the end of that process, just before each box is closed, an employee of the company adds two or three packets more, just for good measure. "I couldn't sleep at night if one of our customers accidentally got a box with 98 or 99 packets inside," says Eisenstadt.

There couldn't be much better PR for a company than that. People don't usually think a lot about their sweetener and often use whatever's at hand or buy what's on sale at the supermarket. But after having seen this piece, I feel that I know and admire the owner of this company. I know that I will be a loyal Sweet 'N Low customer from now on.

5. Direct Marketing

Direct marketing is a measurable, tested marketing method whereby products or services are offered to a targeted audience and a direct response is solicited. Direct marketing encompasses the following:

- Direct mail programs—anything you mail out to people in which you're asking them to order something from you or to respond to you in some way
- Direct response print advertising—any ad that includes a telephone order number, a coupon, or an order form for response
- Direct response television—any ad or infomercial that includes a telephone number or address to mail in orders
- Direct response radio—any ad that includes a telephone number or address to mail in orders
- The Internet—any Web site in which people are asked to place an order (or that gives a telephone number to call to place an order)

Direct marketing can be one of the most effective tools of Friendship Branding because it allows you to talk to customers one-on-one. Not long ago, we all had one-on-one relationships with the people who sold us goods and services. We knew the owner of the grocery store on the corner, the barber on Main Street, the one lawyer in town, and the person who delivered milk right to our doorstep.

Most of these stores and services no longer exist. They've been replaced by malls that all look the same, by giant chain stores, by catalogs, home shopping channels, and Internet buying sites. Although we enjoy the convenience, we miss the old-fashioned human connection.

Direct marketing can return some of that human feeling. For one thing, mail can be personalized so that you're actually

writing to your customer by name (which is why it's so important to get that name right). Dale Carnegie, famous for his
book *How to Win Friends and Influence People,* said that a
person's name is the sweetest sound in the English language
to that person. Therefore, when you use a person's name in
a mail piece, it makes the person have a warmer feeling
toward you. For another, it is possible in many instances to
learn a lot about each individual customer and to address his
or her needs directly. Amazon.com does that when it recommends books, music, or videos to customers who have purchased from them before.

6. Outbound Telemarketing

Outbound telemarketing occurs when a company calls
current or potential customers for the purpose of making a
sale. This is actually part of a direct marketing campaign,
but I made it a separate category here because it is very
often the first impression a customer will have of your company or brand. It is truly reaching out to touch your customers, in the privacy of their own homes. Although most
people will tell you they hate telemarketing, it is an effective
sales tool. If it didn't work, companies would stop using it.
Although it is expensive to set up and maintain, there is a
much higher response to telemarketing than there is to
direct mail.

If people hate telemarketing as much as they say they do
and always say no whenever they're called, why do brands
persist in using this form of marketing? The interesting thing
about telemarketing is that most people don't remember who
called them. They might remember getting a call, especially if
the person is particularly rude or annoying, but for the most

part, they forget who called almost immediately and, so, are not alienated from the brand.

Many people (especially the elderly) respond to telemarketers because they are lonely and are looking to make human connections. That's why they're so susceptible to telemarketing fraud. But done well and honestly, telemarketing can be a perfect Friendship Branding tool. There is a great opportunity for marketers who really understand their product and the people they are calling. Unfortunately, many telemarketers do not take that opportunity.

Suppose that you were given my name by a friend. You call me up at an inconvenient hour, mispronounce my name, immediately go into a monolog telling me all about yourself (while it's clear you don't know a thing about me), and don't let me get a word in edgewise. Why would I want to be your friend?

The problem is that telemarketers are not given the time or training for Friendship Branding. They are not interested in serving customers' needs. They are given a script to read and a quota of calls to make. Any deviation and they are at risk of losing their jobs. Telemarketing is viewed as a numbers game—call enough people and you're bound to get a certain number who will say yes. What would happen if telemarketers were trained to treat you as if they were friends calling to recommend a product or service to you that you might really need? Or what if they called to find out whether you were happy about a product you bought from them?

If telemarketing is effective now simply because of the enormous number of calls that are made, think of how much more effective it could be if Friendship Branding was added to the equation.

7. Inbound Telemarketing

Inbound telemarketing occurs when a customer calls a company to make a purchase or inquiry in response to a direct marketing effort. Here is another area in which first impressions are of utmost importance. (Technically, this may actually be a second impression, because callers are responding to some kind of offer they have seen or heard, whether it be a catalog, a direct mail or direct response offer, an infomercial, and so on.)

Here's an example of "unfriendly branding": Not too long ago, my friend Sheila saw a clothes steamer advertised on a home shopping channel and decided to place an order. She could see from the on-screen count that many viewers were making this purchase, so she was prepared to be put on hold for a few minutes. However, she was not prepared to hear the following recorded announcement: "Our phone lines are extremely busy right now. If you have your membership number ready, please stay on the line. If you are a first-time shopper, please hang up and call back again later."

Call back later! She couldn't believe they were too busy to take her money. She did not purchase the steamer, or any other product from them. She understood that it takes longer to set up an account for someone dialing in for the first time than to take an order from a current customer. But she felt that she was being dismissed and that it wasn't important to the company that she become a customer. Who knows? She might have become one of their best buyers. But because she was treated rudely, she won't call again.

When you telephone a busy friend, she doesn't ask you to make the call again. She says, "I can't talk right now. Can I call you back later?" You understand that she's busy; you don't feel as if you've been brushed off. If this shopping network wanted to create a relationship with Sheila, they could have handled the situation another way, treating new shoppers the way we treat our friends. Instead of asking them to call back, the same recorded announcement might have ended by saying, "If you are a first-time shopper, please leave your name and telephone number after the beep, and one of our operators will call you back within half an hour."

8. Retail

Sam Walton had one of the best ideas ever when he installed greeters at the door of each Wal-Mart store. This is definitely the way to make friends and to let people know that they will be welcome any time they stop by. It used to be that only the more upscale stores like Bloomingdale's and Saks Fifth Avenue had greeters, and they often gave off more snob appeal than Friendship Branding. But Sam Walton makes sure that his greeters are cheerful and helpful and welcoming.

There are many elements that contribute to the Friendship Branding of a retail location, including the layout of the store, the merchandise displays, the cleanliness of the premises (including the restrooms), and the attitude and product knowledge of the employees.

Successful retail is in the details. It's the details that count where retail is concerned. When customers go to the mall, they hop (and shop) easily from one store to another, from one retail experience to the next. As a retailer, you're inviting customers into your "home." They are your guests. They expect to feel welcome, to be treated courteously. So, if your hospitality is lacking, or if they are not as well looked after as they feel they should be, customers will not visit your home again.

The retail experience should also be fun. For instance, the Fairway food market in New York City has one section of the store that's completely devoted to meat, fish, and other refrigerated items. Instead of putting these items behind glassed-in counters, they have them openly displayed in a giant meat locker that customers can walk into! And because it's so cold, the store provides parkas for anyone who wants one so that customers can shop in comfort no matter how cold the meat locker gets.

Another example comes from another food market, this one from Stew Leonard's, "The World's Largest Dairy Store." This business started in 1924, when Charles Leo Leonard began bottling milk in his barn and delivering it by horse and wagon. Stew Leonard took over the business from his father, and in 1969, he opened a large store in Norwalk, Connecticut. Included was a dairy plant in the center of the store, where customers could watch milk being bottled right before their eyes.

Stew Leonard's, with sales approaching $250 million, has been built on two concepts: fun and customer service. The fun comes as soon as you walk in the door. There's an in-store bakery that wafts delicious bread and cake scents throughout the store. There's "The Farm Fresh Five," state-of-the-art audio-animatronic robots who perform original songs about milk and about shopping at Stew Leonard's (see Figure 6.1). And there are the employees, dressed as cows, chickens, and ducks, who stroll the aisles to amuse customers and their children.

As for customer service, the foundation of Stew Leonard's is pleasing the customer. At the store's entrance, a three-ton "Rock of Commitment" displays the store's credo:

Figure 6.1   The "Farm Fresh Five" animatronic robots add to the fun of shopping at Stew Leonard's stores.

"RULE #1: The customer is always right. RULE #2: If the customer is ever wrong, re-read rule #1!"

9. The Internet

Yesterday I wanted to introduce a colleague to a Web site that I had visited a few times and found interesting. Unfortunately, we had a difficult time getting there. Perhaps my colleague has a slow computer. Whatever the reason, it took several long minutes for the site to load. He soon lost interest. When the home page finally did come up, the first thing he saw was a huge banner ad for someone else's Web site.

At first, we weren't even sure if we were on the right page. It was like going to visit a friend and being greeted at the door by a complete stranger. The ad made us think the site we were visiting was more interested in making money from its advertising partner than in making us feel welcome.

Other sites are a lot more welcoming. Their home page is clear, with a simple welcoming message and a map to get around the site in case you've never been there before. They make it easy for visitors to get around and then to make a buying decision should they choose to do so.

One of the biggest problems with Internet branding at this stage of its development is that it is not always consistent with the brand as a whole. This is often because the site was designed either by a division that is totally separate from the rest of the company or by a young person fresh out of school who doesn't yet have any marketing experience. In the latter case, the Web site ends up with a much "younger" feel to it, one that doesn't match the brand's original advertising or promotion image. When a Web site doesn't match the image of the brand, consumers often get confused, and their impression is that the brand is confused about its own identity.

A brand *is* the impression it makes to its customers. There is no real tangible "brand" that you can hold in your hand and use. It's all in the customer's mind. A brand is like a promise, and it's just as fragile. If a brand breaks a promise, it betrays the person to whom the promise was made. If a brand gives a false or deceptive impression, it betrays its customers.

On the other hand, customers will keep buying from a company if it keeps its promises, exceeds its customers expectations, and focuses on creating a consistent impression of Friendship Branding.

Chapter Summary

- A good impression is like a promise made. If the impression lasts, the promise is kept, and a friendship is born. If the impression is false or misleading, the promise is broken and the potential for friendship disappears.

- There are nine ways to make an impression with your product or service:

1. Word of mouth
2. Advertising
3. Promotion
4. Public relations
5. Direct marketing
6. Outbound telemarketing
7. Inbound telemarketing
8. Retail
9. The Internet

Friendship is born at that moment when one person says to another, "What! You too? I thought I was the only one."

—C. S. Lewis

Chapter Seven

Stage Three: How to Connect with the Right Customers

There are millions and millions of people in the world. Out of all those millions of people, each one of us claims a few dozen, at the most, as our true friends. We're careful about whom we choose. We choose people we feel we can trust, people with whom we have something in common. Perhaps it is a shared sense of humor, or a particular political leaning, or a common interest in sports, opera, rock climbing, or rock 'n' roll. Basically, we choose friends who are reflections of ourselves.

Generally, customers connect with brands, companies, and products in much the same way; however, they often connect with companies that are reflections of who and what they would *like to be*, and whose products, services, and brands enhance their lifestyle and image. For example, women who read *Vogue* aspire to the income level and sophistication its advertising conveys. So, some of your customers want to be your friend right now; others look forward to forming a friendship later on, when their economic or social status has grown.

But as a brand, you can't just sit and wait for customers to go looking for new friends. You have to seek out customers. You have to know what kinds of people would want to be friends with you. You have to know who you want to be your friends—and you have to know where to look for them.

Finding Your "Friends"

There are many techniques a company of any size can select and use to target customers with the Friendship Branding focus. Following are four of them.

1. Go Vertical

Not so long ago, brands (except for a few "specialty" brands that appealed only to a few interested consumers, such as sports enthusiasts or gourmet cooks) tried to be all things to all people. Their approach, in advertising, promotions, and direct mail, was an impersonal appeal to the mass market. The idea was to talk to as many people as possible, as often as possible, and hope that your message got through. In fact, some still use this approach. But it is not always cost effective.

Not only do consumers have many more options than they ever had before, but brand advertisers do too. Think about television advertising. Not so long ago, you had only a few factors to consider. There were the basic three national networks—ABC, NBC, and CBS. There might be one or two local stations from which to choose in every market. And that was it. Now there are HUNDREDS of stations in every market, most geared toward specific interests such as cooking, sports, women, movie classics, romance movie classics, science fiction, comedy, children's programming, nostalgic television shows, fishing, gardening, home improvement, home shopping—the list goes on, and on, and on.

So now television advertisers are able to target specific markets. For instance, any brand geared toward women would probably do well advertising on Lifetime Television (for women), beer would do well on ESPN, and health products on American Movie Classics (which is geared toward older people). These are known as *vertical markets,* and they are dedicated to a specific field or interest.

Take numismatists, for example. They collect coins. There is a magazine called *Coin Age,* dedicated to information about coins and coin collecting. There are basically two types of ads in this magazine. One is geared toward the serious coin collector and offers proof sets and un-circulated coins, terms that sophisticated collectors understand. The other ads are geared toward stamps. Apparently, numismatists are often also philatelists.

Another example of a vertical market is *Diabetes Forecast Magazine.* When the marketers of the *Diabetes Weight Loss System* book were looking for their customers, the most logical place to put their ad was in a magazine that many diabetics read (see Figure 7.1). The ad, designed by Tedd Appel of Market Development Group in Washington, D.C., targets those people who are most in need of the information

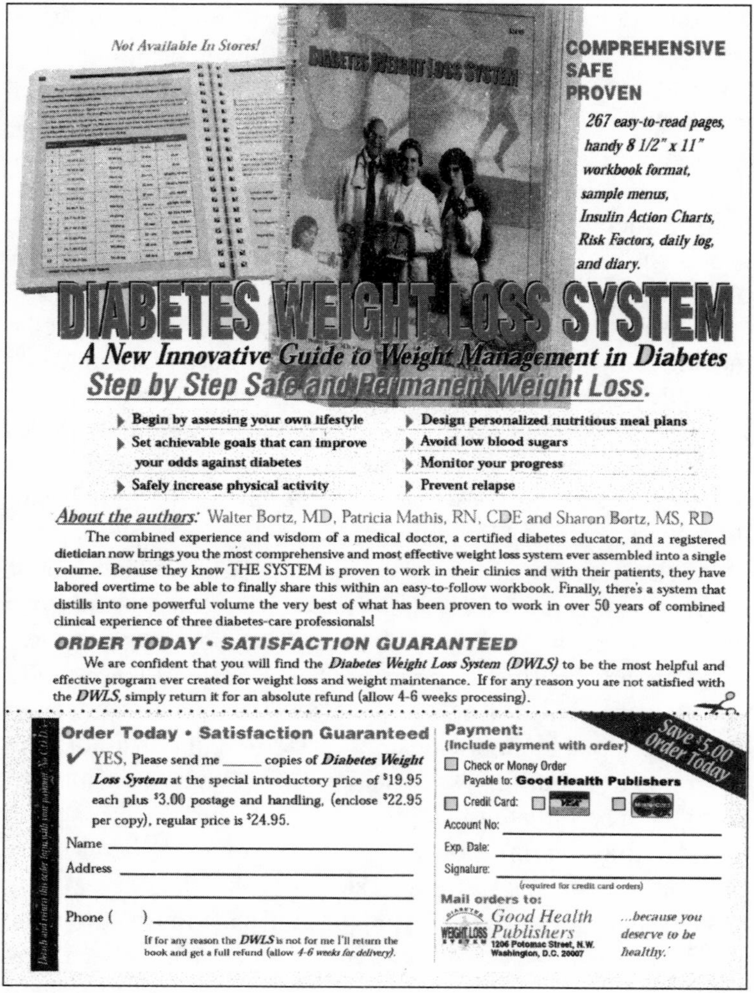

Figure 7.1   This ad was placed in a tightly targeted magazine to
appeal to a very specific customer base.

contained in this book. So the ad is not only bringing in customers but also helping diabetics locate a product they are likely to want and need.

The most important thing about advertising in a vertical publication is that there is an inferred endorsement of your product by the magazine or newspaper. I am a collector of coins, and I do trust (whether naively or not) that *Coin Age* won't accept ads from a disreputable dealer. I'm sure that readers of *Diabetes Forecast Magazine* feel the same way about that publication.

2. Go Broad

There are other times when you want to broaden your circle of friends. Perhaps the market you have been targeted is saturated. That's what happened to a small vitamin company in upstate New York. They had been successfully marketing a product for seniors for many years but felt it had saturated that market. Research told them that adding calcium to the vitamin made it beneficial to younger women as well. By modifying the product (along with the advertising and promotion), the company was able to appeal to a broader market and extend the life of the product.

Even companies that would seem at first glance to have a narrow appeal sometimes choose to go for a broader audience. Take the coins we spoke about earlier, for instance. You'll sometimes see coin sets advertised in FSIs (Free Standing Inserts) in Sunday papers and supplements. These sets (usually all the coins of a particular year) are not really meant for the serious collector. People who buy these sets do so to mark the date of a child's birth or perhaps as a gift to get someone started collecting.

The same goes for baseball cards. Although it would seem that the best place to advertise these would be in sports magazines and newspapers, special editions often have a broader appeal. Joseph England, veteran direct marketing entrepreneur and creator of hundreds of successful direct response ads, including one for Mark McGwire's historic home runs (see Figure 7.2), says: "These cards do well when they are advertised in newspapers like *USA Today* and Sunday supplements like *Parade* because they appeal to such a huge number of people—even those who are not ordinarily sports fans.

Figure 7.2 This ad for Mark McGwire baseball cards was placed in broad-based newspapers to appeal to as wide an audience as possible.

3. Go Direct

For many years, direct marketing has been the leading method of finding friends in all the right places. Both direct response advertising and direct mail have been striving for years to narrow their focus on specific audiences. As a marketer, the more you know about an individual consumer, the easier it is to develop offers that will appeal to her.

For instance, if you know how old a consumer is, you can choose either to include him in your mailing list (if you are selling rap music, for instance, and the consumer is a young adult) or eliminate him (if he is a baby boomer, who is not likely be interested in rap music). As technology has advanced, these audiences are getting narrower all the time.

In Friendship Branding, there are two purposes to targeting narrow audiences. First, it helps you find customers likely to buy from you. Second, it is a gesture of friendship. We depend on our friends to know what we like and to let us know when they find something they think will interest us. I collect porcelain figurines stamped "Made in Occupied Japan." Whenever any of my friends come across such a piece, they either buy it for me or let me know where they saw it so that I can take a look at it myself.

I also subscribe to *Coin Age* magazine. Being a subscriber to this magazine gives me information about and access to special coins that would be difficult to find elsewhere. I want legitimate coin dealers to seek me out by placing their advertising in a magazine they know I'm going to read. I appreciate the fact that when I'm in the market to buy coins, I have a specific, and trustworthy, place to find them. The more specific a brand can get in terms of knowing its customers, the closer the friendships it can make.

For instance, in 1998, Bloomingdale's department store segmented its more than 55 million customers into 550 distinct categories and created customized advertising or direct marketing for each one. This allowed them to target not only their best customers but also their marginal audiences (e.g., lapsed customers).

"By treating them special, and sending them a unique offer, we can reactivate these customers at a profitable response rates," says Vice President of Marketing Susan J. Harvey. "And as a result of more precisely targeted mailings, our ROI has improved by as much as 30% in many cases."

Direct marketers are able to narrowly segment customers through choosing the most appropriate mailing lists and by making the most appropriate selections from those lists. For instance, Mason & Geller recently designed a direct mail piece to get new subscribers for a popular fishing magazine aimed at a specific type of fishing enthusiast. Here are some of the list choices and selections (categories you choose in order to focus on your target audience) they made for this mailing:

List	Selection
Baseball Digest	Subscribers
College and Pro Football Weekly	Subscribers
Inside Sports	Subscribers
Sports Illustrated	Subscribers
Anheuser-Busch Catalog	Last 6 Mos. Buyers
ESPN Home Videos	Last 12 Mos. Buyers
Babe Ruth Baseball League	Men, Ages 17 and 18
College Bound Student	Men/Baseball/Basketball
Florida License Holder	Buyers
Fishing Boat Owners	ME, NH, MA, RI, CT, NY, NJ, MD, DE, VA, NC, SC, GA, FL, CA

4. Go Creative

If you're unhappy with the friends you have or feel that you need to meet "new kinds" of people, you can't just keep visiting your old haunts. You have to come up with some new places to find people you might like.

Sometimes it pays to be creative when you're looking for new customers as well. If you're selling exotic imported high-end jewelry, you're first instinct would probably be to advertise in upscale magazines that cater to wealthy subscribers (e.g., *Saveur* and *Architectural Digest*) and to consider renting mailing lists from high-end retail stores like Saks Fifth Avenue and Tiffany's. However, you may be missing out on potential customers by limiting your creative thinking.

This may be a good time to analyze your current customer base. What do your customers have in common besides the fact that they can afford expensive jewelry? If you let your mind go and try a little free association, you might come up with some unusual—but effective—sources for new prospects.

What about advertising in *Travel & Leisure,* a magazine that world travelers enjoy? People who are interested in exotic locales may also be interested in products from those locales. And what about renting the mailing list of people who have ordered from museum catalogs? They, too, are interested in the unusual and may be good targets for your company. And if you rented a museum's list, you could select zip codes known to be areas where the wealthy reside.

Finding Your "Best" Friends

If you were on a serious quest to find new friends, you wouldn't just approach a crowd of strangers and shout,

"Anybody want to be my friend?" Chances are, you would get one or two replies. But then you would have to ask yourself some questions: Who are these people? Why do they want to be my friend? Will they stick around for a while, or are they only in it for curiosity's sake? And what do they have in common with the friends I already have? The truth is, we always want to find friends that are similar to our present group. These are the kinds of people who appreciate us, who "get" our sense of humor, who will stick by us in times of trouble. So even though we're looking for new friends, we don't want them to be all that different from the ones we have.

When brands use the "anybody want to be my friend" approach to finding new customers, they, too, will get a response. But these are not necessarily customers who will stick around, continue buying, and remain loyal. You want new customers, but you want them to be similar to the ones who are buying from you now. Do you know who your present customers are? Do you know the people most likely to buy your product or service in the future?

Take a few minutes and visualize your ideal customer. Don't try to visualize thousands of people; create an image of just one person. That's the person you're trying to reach. That's the person you want for your friend, and that's the person with whom you want to connect.

What's the best way to connect with someone? Learn as much as you can about them. Anticipate their needs and wants. There are three main ways to do this.

Study Your Customers' Statistics

In order to know how best to appeal to future buyers for your brand, you need to paint a picture of your ideal customer. The easiest way to start this process is to consider the *demographics*. Demographics is defined as measurable statistics of population, in other words, the facts that describe a specific group of people. These facts include:

Sex: Does your brand appeal more to men or women? Both?

Age: Is your customer likely to be under twenty? Over fifty? Entering college? Reaching retirement? Somewhere in between?

Income: If you're selling an expensive product or service, your customers probably needs an income level high enough to be able to afford what you're offering. You don't want to waste your time offering a $2,000 fine art print to someone who can't afford to spend that much (unless you're offering flexible payment terms).

To maximize use of demographics, you must picture your customer in your mind and make a list of attributes that fit her ethnicity, education, income, place of residence, and number of children. If your brand appeals to the business customer, you must have the same clear picture of what that customer is like, including the nature of the business, the geographic location of the business, the size of the company, the number of employees, the business's sales volume, or other criteria.

Using these demographics can help you select the most appropriate markets and media in which to advertise your brand, whether it is radio, television, magazines, newspapers, or direct mail.

Study Your Customers' Behavior

Another feature in the portrait of your ideal customer is how she thinks and, therefore, behaves. This is known as *psychographics* and refers to the type of person who is likely to buy your brand. Psychographics refer to lifestyle and attitude as opposed to the hard facts of demographics. Psychographics can include such things as values, conservative vs. liberal leaning, stage in life (single, full nest, empty nest, etc.), interests, hobbies, motivations (status, principles, etc.).

As much as we would like to think so, not everyone is going to be equally interested in your product or service. Every brander wants to answer "everybody," but that is not usually the case. There are probably certain groups of people that are more likely than others to want what you have to offer. For instance, it may be a product that will appeal to men who enjoy hunting, or it may be something that is perfect for women who are juggling family and career.

Knowing where your customers live, how old they are, or how much money they make is important, but it isn't enough. You must look at what motivates your customers— their values, behaviors, and beliefs.

Perhaps the greatest breakthrough in attaining psychographic information is the Internet. Because of the technology involved, companies can gather information about their "customers" (in this case, Web site visitors) instantaneously. An article in the September 6, 1999, issue of *Adweek* profiled Larry Kruguer, vice president of marketing at SportsLine USA, who helped his company "build a storehouse of more than 1 million consumer profiles" to help target specific offers to specific customers.

It's clear that Internet marketers are all racing to gather this important information—to track where people go on the Web, which ads they click on, and what they buy.

In the case of SportsLine, the company uses the information to run offers for merchandise tailored to a viewer's past behavior at the site. "Consumers pegged as New York Mets fans, for instance," says Vonder Haar, "may see customized offers for Mets merchandise even when they are reading a story about the division rival Atlanta Braves."

Changes in society over the past several decades in work style and family life have significantly increased the complexity of the marketplace. From politics to microbreweries, consumers are spinning off into tighter and tighter buying circles. The more you know about your target audience, the better able you are to create and place advertising that will influence their purchasing behavior.

Add in the Customer Focus Factor

The third way to anticipate your customers' needs and wants is to add in the customer focus factor. You do that by constantly asking yourself this one questions: What can we do to make our customers' lives easier?

First, you can personalize your offers. Take a hint from Amazon.com, when it recommends products that match your interests, or from SportsLine USA, when it makes offers to customers based on past purchases. If you don't yet have the technology to make such specifically personalized offers, you can still make customers feel special in other ways. Take the example of httprint *(www.httprint.com),* a new company that produces a Web site designed for businesses that use printers and printing services. According to their marketing materials,

Figure 7.3 Httprint sent out this adorable personalized mailing to get me to go to their booth at a Direct Marketing Association trade show. It worked.

Figure 7.4 Httprint ran a contest at the trade show. In order to win, you had to visit their booth to drop off your entry. But the possibility of winning this scooter was too hard to resist.

their Web site makes it possible to "find anything and every-thing related to printing and direct marketing production."

When the company wanted to draw prospects to their booth at a recent Direct Marketing Association trade show in Toronto, it sent out a cute, clever, personalized invitation. It's personalized because it's addressed specifically to me, Lois (see Figure 7.3). It even shows me riding on a scooter I can win if I go to their booth and enter their contest (see Figure 7.4). This was the launch of their brand, and this mailing piece told me many things about them. It told me they were smart (I am absolutely the right target for their services), it told me they were interested in finding out more about me (the mailer included a brief survey to get more information), and they were fun (as demonstrated by the great cartoon drawings throughout). This is brand that made me feel, before I ever had any dealings with it, that it would be a great friend to have.

The second way is to add unexpected free or low-cost services that customers can enjoy. For example, 1-800-FLOWERS allows customers to send free virtual bouquets via e-mail (see Figure 7.5). It's a great way to get customers coming back to their Web site again and again. And it makes sense that when they are ready to send a *real* bouquet, the brand they will think of first will be 1-800-FLOWERS.

These unexpected surprises don't have to be ongoing (if they are, they become expected). But a little something extra for a holiday is always nice. This is something that Lisa Roland has done with 1-800-PETFOOD. "I think everyone likes treats and surprises," says Roland, "so we try to do something unexpected every so often. Last Halloween, for instance, all of our customers' dogs got a big rawhide bone tied with

Figure 7.5 It's an unexpected treat to be able to send a FREE virtual greeting to someone via 1-800-FLOWERS.

ribbon, and customers' cats got a bag of Whisker Lickins' cat food. Each one had a bright orange tag hanging from it that said, 'It's spooky how much we love having you as a customer. Here's a treat. We'll leave the tricks to you.'"

1-800-PETFOOD

Imagine that you're coming home on a cold winter's night after a busy day at work, looking forward to settling in, all warm and cozy with your two pets, Tyrone (the dog) and Harley (the cat). You open the door, and you're greeted happily and slurpily. You fling off your coat, kick off your shoes, and get ready to feed the "kids." But when you get to the cabinet—no food! You were supposed to stop at the store on the way home, and you completely forgot.

What would you do? If you were Lisa Roland of New York City, you'd help create a company to take care of such problems. Realizing that New Yorkers (and people all across the United States) were tired of making late night trips to the store and lugging home all those heavy bags filled with cans and boxes of pet food and supplies, she teamed up with Mitchell's, The World's Finest Newspaper Delivery Service, a company that has delivered newspapers and beverages to New Yorkers for more than fifty years. Using the easy-to-remember phone number 1-800-PETFOOD, their idea was to deliver pet-related items right to owners' doorsteps.

1-800-PETFOOD's first task was to figure out the best way to reach potential customers. How could they identify the consumer population most likely to respond to their offer? How could they find out who in this vast city had cats and dogs?

The company first sent out a survey to 50,000 Mitchell's customers asking about their pets. As an incentive to fill out the survey, they created a contest whereby five respondents would win $100 toward their next Mitchell's bill just for answering their questions.

Survey questions included the following: Do you have a dog? Do you have a cat? If yes, how many do you have? What are their names? What are their breeds? How old are they? What do you currently feed them? Where do you currently buy their food?

"We were trying to determine what percentage of the population had pets," says Roland, director of marketing for the company. "We wanted to know what percentage of owners had multiple pets and how old these pets were so that we could determine what kind of lifetime value we could expect.

We also asked people what they spent each week on pet food and supplies so that we could gauge their annual expenditure. That was also, of course, the beginning of our database."

Once this database of Mitchell's customers was established, 1-800-PETFOOD sent out their first mailing targeted to pet owners. But Roland also knew she'd have to look for other customers to keep the company growing. So the company began experimenting with various ways of marketing, some narrowly targeted and others that reach a broader audience. Following are some of these methods:

> *Teaming up with "host beneficiaries":* These are people who provide pet-related services in the community, such as veterinarians, groomers, trainers, breeders, and shelters. 1-800-PETFOOD provides them with brightly colored discount coupons, which they distribute to their customers, worth $10 off a pet owner's first purchase (see Figure 7.6). "It's a value-add for the host beneficiary," says Roland, "and we get their implied endorsement as well."

> *Teaming up with rescue organizations:* The $10 coupons are also given out to every person who adopts a pet from one of the city's rescue organization. 1-800-PETFOOD then makes a donation back to the organization when a customer makes his or her first purchase.

> *Advertising in targeted magazines and newspapers:* 1-800-PETFOOD advertises in magazines and newspapers that are distributed in various buildings and neighborhoods throughout New York City. One magazine, *We Deliver,* lists menus from restaurants that make

Figure 7.6 This $10-off coupon from 1-800-PETFOOD gives first-time customers a discount—and gets an implied endorsement from the "host beneficiary."

deliveries. Since pets have to eat too, it made perfect sense to advertise in this publication (see Figure 7.7).

Sending out flyers: When a potential customer requests information about 1-800-PETFOOD, they receive a flyer (designed by Mason & Geller) and a $10 coupon (see Figure 7.8). The company also takes the personal approach and hands out flyers at dog runs, street fairs, and other special events.

Sponsoring shopping mall information lines: To broaden their market, the company sponsors information lines at various malls in New Jersey and suburban New York. When shoppers call to get information about directions to the mall, store hours, and so on, they hear, "Welcome to the XYZ Shopping Mall, sponsored by 1-800-PETFOOD. For more information about 1-800-PETFOOD, dial 1; for mall hours dial 2 . . ."

Figure 7.7 This ad ran in the "We Deliver" guides distributed throughout the Upper East and Upper West Sides of Manhattan— 1-800-PETFOOD's target areas.

1-800-PETFOOD is being built on the concepts of Friend-ship Branding. "I know that what we're selling is a commodity item that people can get anywhere," says Roland. "But I know what I want as the 'mom' of a cat and a dog. So we're treating our customers the way we want to be treated. We're creating a 'warm and fuzzy' environment where people and their pets are celebrated."

In order to introduce people to that environment, the company has to explore many avenues of advertising and promotion, both narrow and broad. "When we spend

Figure 7.8 These flyers are distributed wherever people might have pets, and they feature a free treat canister with home-baked goodies for cats or dogs.

money," Roland says, "we spend it either somewhere like the veterinarians' offices, where we know pet owners are likely to be, or somewhere like the shopping malls—where the CPM [cost per thousand] is just irresistible."

If you want your brand to survive long term, you need a long-term approach to finding customers. That means studying your present customer base, analyzing as much data as you can obtain, and then making your customers feel special and valued by personalizing offers directly to them. That's a sure way to find friends who will follow you anywhere!

Chapter Summary

- Techniques to target customers include these:

  1. Go vertical: Try specialized publications or events dedicated to specific fields or interests related to your brand.
  2. Go broad: Reach out to a broader audience in order to extend the life of your brand.
  3. Go direct: Use direct marketing techniques to segment your database and create unique offers for your segmented customers.
  4. Go creative: Try brainstorming and free association to find untapped sources of new customers.

- Visualize your ideal customer by creating an image of just one person, the person you want for your friend.

- Anticipate your customers' wants and needs via demographics and psychographics.

- Add in the customer focus factor:

  Answer this question: What can we do to make customers' lives easier?

  Personalize your offers.

  Add unexpected free or low-cost services.

To hear complaints with patience, even when complaints are vain, is one of the duties of friendship.

—Dr. Samuel Johnson

Chapter Eight

Stage Four: Listening to Your Customers

What is the golden rule of branding? Listening to your customers. They will tell you what they like about your product . . . and more important, what they don't.

There is no greater compliment that you can pay a friend than to say, "You're a good listener." We all appreciate someone who listens to us. I know that there are times in my life when I'm angry or upset about something, and I just have to get whatever is bothering me off my chest. After venting for a few minutes, I feel much better and am able to sincerely say, "Thank you for listening."

But it's not just when I'm angry that I expect my friends to "listen." Listening involves more than just hearing what I say. I expect that my friends know a lot about me, and they notice when things are wrong. I expect that they appreciate the time I spend with them and realize when I haven't called in a while. I want to know that they value my friendship.

Listening is also an important skill for a company to cultivate. But companies often let policy matters and administrative hierarchy put up barriers (real or imaginary) that stand in the way of getting up close and personal with their customers. These barriers can be broken simply by listening to their own customers. There are three major advantages to listening to your customers:

1. Listening makes people feel special and cared about.
2. Listening alerts you to problems or opportunities that you didn't know existed.
3. Listening builds relationships and develops rapport, trust, and understanding.

One company that is particularly adept at listening is Club Med. Prospective customers who call for information talk to well-trained, knowledgeable service representatives. They ask customers for specific information about themselves. For example, they may ask questions such as these: Are you taking this vacation by yourself? With friends? With family? What kind of sports do you enjoy? Do you enjoy nightlife? Using this information, they recommend the appropriate vacation spot.

Another company that exemplifies the impact of listening skills in Friendship Branding is Dell Computer Corporation, led by the example of its CEO, Michael Dell. He spends a half hour every morning listening to customer calls. He hears when customers tell operators about competitors' product cost and quality. He listens when they call customer service with complaints. If there's a problem, he's the first one to fix it. He welcomes feedback, as he states in a personal letter on Dell's Web site: "Building and retaining customer confidence is a huge part of our success, so I hope you'll take a moment to tell us what you think of our Web site and *let us know* how we can improve it to serve you better."

"Buying a computer from Dell is more than just a purchase," says Dell, "it's the beginning of a relationship in which we do our best to ensure that the total customer experience reflects the highest possible standards of quality and service every step of the way."

What You Learn from Listening

What happens when you don't listen to your customers? You keep doing the same things over again, expecting different results.

A complaining customer can be your best friend. When I worked at Vickers & Benson Direct in Canada, Ford was one of our biggest accounts. In the first mailing we did for them, we sent out a survey asking Ford owners what they wanted in a new car, and we gave them a list of choices. There was also a blank space left for comments.

Boy, did we get comments. We got a lot of compliments about how much people enjoyed driving their Ford cars. But most people figure you already know what you did right with the car. However, they don't think you're aware of what you did wrong. So we also received a lot of negative comments from people who had experienced a variety of problems with their cars.

One man wrote and said that the cold winter months and strong Canadian winds had blown off the cross bar on the letter "F" and the top of the letter "O" in the metal letters that spelled out FORD on the front of the car and that, as a result, he was driving around in a TURD. Strangely enough, most of the correspondence we got was, in fact, weather related; customers didn't think Ford had taken the harsh northern winters into consideration.

Back at headquarters, the Ford executive who had hired us was furious. Why had we opened this can of worms? Now they had to deal with hundreds of upset clients! They told us that we should stop this program immediately and that they were going to find another agency.

Then, Ken Harrigan, the chairman of Ford of Canada at the time, stepped in. He too had read the letters. But instead of firing us, he applauded our efforts.

"For the first time," he said, "we are hearing what our customers have to say about our cars. We're getting real feedback—things we can change, things we can fix. Why would we want to turn off that pipeline?" It was an important lesson learned.

Many companies today have a toll-free number that customers can call to complain about problems and to let off steam if they feel the need. It's also a great way to answer any questions or concerns customers might have.

That's the good news. The bad news is that most companies don't do enough with the information they get over that open line. To be truly effective, you must have a knowledgeable person answering the phone who can resolve a complaint, answer a question, take an order, or provide accurate information. Otherwise, the call can cause more frustration than it solves. A toll-free number is a real opportunity to find out what customers like about your brand, what they don't like, and what you can do about it.

In the Geller Branding Survey, we asked respondents to relate both positive and negative stories they had with particular brands. Several were about experiences with one particular retail chain that has recently tried to revitalize its image. Here are two of the stories we got:

B.T. from Manhattan writes:

> I needed a filter for an air purifier my son had purchased for me at a national department store chain near his home. I live in Manhattan, and the closest branch of that chain is many miles north in Tarrytown. I called that store and asked them if they carried this filter. "Yes we do," said the helpful salesperson, who told me his name was Ben. I cajoled my friend into driving me the forty miles to the store. When we got there, we had to search for someone to help us. When we finally found someone, he said they had no filters in stock. When I said, "But I called and Ben said you had them," no one there had ever heard of Ben. We wasted three hours driving back and forth. I came back without a filter and with the certainty that I'm never shopping at that department store again.

And J.W. from Pennsylvania writes:

> I spent hours on the phone with customer service trying to work out a problem with this department store [the same one as in the story above]. Suddenly I got disconnected. When I called back, they couldn't reconnect me with the person I had been speaking to, there were no notes in the computer from my earlier conversation, and I had to start from the beginning again.

Unfortunately, most companies are afraid to listen to their customers; they don't want to hear the bad news. They see the problems instead of the opportunities. But when David Hochberg, vice president of Lillian Vernon Inc., lectured at the direct marketing class I teach at New York University, he told my students this: "Lillian Vernon's *best customers* are those people who had a problem with an item and had that problem resolved to their satisfaction. In fact, those people who had a positive resolution to their problem came back to buy from the company again and again."

Studies have shown that 63 percent of unhappy customers who do not complain will not buy from you again. But of those who do and have their problems resolved, only 5 percent will not come back. This is borne out by some positive stories we received in our branding surveys, including the following:

S.K. from Philadelphia writes:

> I bought a necklace from one of the home shopping channels, and the clasp was broken when I received it. I asked my friend, who was going to the post office, to return it for me. She did but inadvertently put her return address on the package. I didn't realize this and wondered why I was still being charged on my credit card for an item I had returned. Luckily, my friend had kept her receipt, and I was able to track the package. Since it hadn't had my name on it anywhere, the shopping channel had no idea who it came from. I fully expected that there would be a problem with the refund, since the company had no proof the necklace had come back from me. But they were as nice as could be and immediately arranged to credit my account. I'd shop with them again any time.

And R.P. from New Jersey writes:

I bought a ceiling fan at a large home improvements
store. My husband and I tried to install it, but we just
couldn't get the parts to fit correctly. We went back to the
store with the fan in pieces. Although there was nothing
wrong with the fan (it turned out we were putting it
together incorrectly), the salesperson took it back and
gave us a new one—and offered to come by our home
on his own time the next day to help us install it. That
was service that went way beyond the call of duty and
made us loyal customers of that store.

Getting to Know Your Customers

Although there are many ways of getting to know your customers, not every method is practical for every brand. However, every brand should find a way to hear from its
customers, listen to them, and react.

Before a new brand is introduced, companies go to a lot
of trouble to find the right name, the right design, the right
color, the right flavor, the right . . . whatever . . . to make sure
it appeals to its target audience. They hold focus groups and
introduce the brand into test markets to see what customers'
reactions will be. The company listens intently to try to gauge
the customers' slightest preferences.

But what happens once that brand is introduced? Many
companies simply stop listening. They can judge by the
numbers whether the brand is gaining or losing market
share, but they don't really know why they are gaining or
losing individual buyers. They don't know what customers

like and don't like about their brand. They have closed the "pipeline" that could supply valuable marketing information. Following are five effective ways to keep customer communications open.

1. Database Analysis

Brands that are sold via direct marketing, direct response (in print, television, or radio), catalogs, or e-commerce already have this potent listening tool in place. Database marketing has been in existence for as long as companies have written down the names and addresses of customers for their records. Refining and maintaining your house file and your prospect lists allows you to customize your marketing efforts to those people who are most likely to buy your products.

By using the technology available today, brands can utilize data appending, or overlay, to build a profile of exactly who their customers are, what they're buying, and when. This can help in two ways:

1. It can help you build customer lists. Once you have a model of your "typical" customer, you can find new prospect lists that have customers similar to your own.
2. It can help you segment your own customer list. By segmenting your own customer list, you can target particular products to specific segments of your list. This is what Amazon.com does when it recommends certain categories of books, music, or videos to customers who have noted a preference for or who have previously purchased that type of book, music, or video.

When and Why People Stop Being Your Customers

Did you ever know someone who, without your even noticing, slipped out of your circle of friends? This was not one of your closest friends, perhaps, but someone you used to see quite often at social events. You'd go out to the movies every so often, or to dinner in the neighborhood. Then, you realize you haven't heard from this friend in a while. You know you really should call her, but you get so busy you never call, and you've lost a friend for good.

What happens, though, if you do call and say, "I haven't heard from you in a while. Why don't you come by for dinner next week?" Your friend is probably delighted to hear from you and will gladly accept your invitation. She might explain that she's been busy, too, and has been meaning to call. Or she might just tell you about something you did to offend her, something you were not even aware you did, which is why she has not called.

She could have called to let you know that she was annoyed. But, being human, she was hoping that you'd be the first to notice she was gone. Maybe she was "testing" you to see how much you valued this friendship. This may be unrealistic, but it's often the way we feel.

We want brands to notice too. We want them to notice when we respond to their overtures of friendship and when we stop responding.

I have a friend who loves tea so much so that she even collects antique tea tins. She also had a favorite brand of herbal tea that she used to buy quite often. A few years ago, there was an offer on packages of this tea: Send in three proofs of purchase and $3.95 and the company would send back a collectible tea tin. My friend was thrilled! It couldn't have been a more perfect offer for her. She purchased three boxes of tea, sent in her $3.95, and received an adorable collectible tin.

She never heard from the company again. "I gave up something of value to this brand—my name and address," she told me, "and then I was ignored. I imagined that they were making this offer in order to start a relationship with me, that I would be recognized as one of their loyal customers. But I didn't even get a thank you for buying the tin! I often wondered why they bothered with that promotion. They certainly couldn't have made a fortune from the $3.95 I sent in for the tin. I still buy the tea occasionally, but not as much as I used to."

This brand must have had many thousands of customers who purchased tea tins. Perhaps the company assumed that just getting customers to purchase the three boxes of tea to collect the proofs of purchase would make them loyal customers. But my friend didn't feel that way; she felt ignored. I'm sure most of the other people who sent away for the tin felt that way too. That means many thousands of opportunities to form long-lasting customer friendships were lost because those names were not put into a database for future contact.

Watch Out for Silent Defectors

There is another opportunity for database analysis that is missed by most brands, and that is keeping track of customers who stop buying. Many customers are what I call "silent defectors." There are two main reasons people do not complain when they are dissatisfied. First, they think that their complaint will do no good. They don't believe you'll really listen to what they have to say. And second, they aren't sure how to voice their complaint. Your job is to let your customers know that complaints do make a difference, and to make it easy for them to complain.

I'm often one of those silent defectors. If I am displeased with something I buy, I don't usually return it. Instead I suffer in silence and simply do not buy from that company again.

This is the case with a mail-order brand I used to purchase from regularly, spending several hundred dollars each year. About a year ago, I was dissatisfied with a few items I received. I did not return these items, but it has now been over a year since I've bought anything else from the company. Apparently, they haven't noticed I've defected.

All they'd have to do would be to check their database for people who have stopped buying for at least twelve months. They could send a letter saying, "We want you back," and a coupon for $10 off the next purchase. If they were really smart, they would ask why the customer stopped buying.

You can do that easily with a letter and questionnaire like the ones below.

Dear Ms. Sanders,

We miss you! We noticed that it's been a while since we've heard from you, and we're always concerned when a valued customer stops doing business with us.

It would help us to serve you (and other customers like you) better if you would take a few minutes to tell us about your experiences with our company and answer the questions enclosed. Your input is very important to us.

A postage-paid envelope has been enclosed for your convenience. Thank you for your help, and we hope to be able to serve you again in the future.

Sincerely,
John H. Dunne
President

Questionnaire

How long have you been a customer with us?

What products/services did you purchase from us?

Please indicate the main reasons you stopped doing business with us (check all that apply):
A. Moved from area
B. No longer have need of product or service
C. Poor service
D. An unresolved problem
E. Other (please explain)

Are you now purchasing this product or service from another firm?

If so, with whom?

If you'd like to speak with me personally about this, please feel free to call at (555) 555-5555 or e-mail me at johndunne@brandx.com. Thank you for your input. It is greatly appreciated.

2. Surveys

Everyone loves to be asked for his or her views. There is nothing more flattering than to have a friend call you or send you an e-mail that says, "I need some advice, and I really respect and value your opinion." If you know your friend is sincere, you'll gladly take the time to answer a few questions. Then, of course, you want to keep in touch with that friend to find out whether he or she took your advice.

Surveys are one of the most effective and underutilized methods of listening to customers. And now, with the major technological advances of the Internet, they are relatively easy to conduct. Every brand's Internet site should include a survey. Most now include an e-mail address for customers to contact the company directly. Why not include a survey as well? It could be set up in a multiple-choice or fill-in-the-blank format.

A beverage brand might include the following questions:

1. On a scale of 1-5 (5 being best), rate our product?
   A. 1   C. 3   E. 5
   B. 2   D. 4
2. Which flavor do you buy most often?
   A. Iced tea   D. Pineapple orange
   B. Passion fruit   E. Strawberry mango
   C. Vanilla cream   F. Apple peach
3. What flavor(s) would you like us to offer (circle as many as apply)?
   A. Chocolate   D. Cranberry apple
   B. Cranberry juice   E. Grapefruit
   C. Tangerine   F. Cinnamon tea
4. Where do you buy our product most often?
   A. Supermarket   C. Vending machine
   B. Convenience store
5. What other brands do you buy?
   A. Snapple   C. Very Fine
   B. Arizona tea

You can ask customers any questions that will help you understand who they are and what their preferences are. You can also use the survey for market research purposes—to let you know what customers would like to see next from your brand.

This kind of survey doesn't have to be done on the Internet, of course. It can be done through the mail as well. Mosby Matthew Bender (a publisher of medical books that is no longer in business) wanted to find out what had happened to some of their silent defectors. So they checked their database for customers who had not purchased books for the past several years. Then they sent them a letter saying, "We need your help to serve you better!" and asked them to take part in a survey (see Figure 8.1). The survey gave these lapsed customers an opportunity to tell Mosby which areas of medicine they were interested in so that Mosby could send them targeted mailings. As a friendly gesture, the company offered $5 off the customer's next purchase. This mailing received a huge response from Mosby's lapsed customers, who quickly used the certificate to purchase books.

There are, however, pros and cons to mailed surveys. Mailed surveys allow your company to ask more detailed questions that encourage longer answers. Respondents can often take more time with mailed surveys and fill them out at their leisure. However, there are drawbacks to mailed surveys as well. Response rates are not always high. Also, the respondent may send back an incomplete survey, which may invalidate that response. (If you're conducting a survey on the Internet, you can send an immediate message that says, "Survey cannot be submitted because

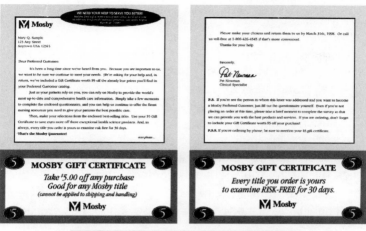

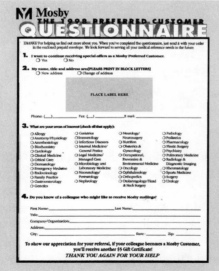

Figure 8.1 This survey and $5 gift certificate sent to Mosby's lapsed customers garnered an excellent response.

question no. 6 has not been answered." You can't do that with a mailed survey.)

There is another type of survey that is currently being used by several brands, and that is to ask questions not of silent defectors but of those customers who make their dissatisfaction known by returning an item. The object is to find out *why* particular items are being returned. Many clothing catalogs, for instance, include surveys on their packing slips along with instructions for returning items. Customers are asked to check off the reason the item is being returned (size, color, fabric, mistake in order, etc.). This is what one of our Geller Branding Survey respondents had to say about this practice:

> I bought a skirt that looked great in the catalog. When I received it in the mail, though, the fabric was rough and scratchy and didn't look like the picture at all. So I returned it. I was glad to see there was a box I could check off to let the company know I was returning the skirt because of the fabric. Even though I was not pleased with the item, it made me feel better knowing they were asking for my opinion. And it gave me a "sliver of hope" that if enough people checked off the box marked "fabric" as the reason for return, maybe the company would do something about it.

It's that sliver of hope that keeps customers relating to the brand. They're watching and waiting to see if anyone responds.

3. Outbound Telemarketing
Current customers, lapsed customers, and new prospects can also be surveyed on the phone. Done well, a telephone interview enables you to gather in-depth information about

what customers like and don't like, and about why they may
have left. Telephone companies do this all the time. The
problem is they don't do it well.

If you switch long-distance carriers, within a few days you
will get a phone call from your original carrier, asking why you
switched and offering you an incentive to switch back. Most of
the time these efforts do not work. For instance, when I
recently changed service, my original carrier called and
offered me $15 to switch back. My average phone bill is sev-
eral hundred dollars a month, so $15 is just not enough of an
incentive. The telemarketer had no authority to offer anything
else, so when I said "No," she had no option but to say,
"Thank you anyway," and hang up.

Why does this happen? Usually it's because a large corporation has hired a telemarketing firm for this important job. The
people calling customers don't work for the brand; they work
for the telemarketing company. They may not even be familiar
with the product they are calling about. They are reading from
a script and can't deal with any problems that may arise. So if
a customer raises an objection they can't answer (because it's
not on the script), they have no choice but to hang up.

Telemarketers represent your brand. This is a simple concept; yet many companies don't invest the funds necessary to
train these representatives correctly. Their job is to help the
brand get and keep loyal customers, but without proper
training, they often end up alienating the very people they are
hired to woo.

4. Focus Groups
Many brands use focus groups to listen to their customers. A focus group is a number of individuals selected

usually by demographic characteristics to participate in a discussion about a certain brand or product. There is a moderator or leader who conducts the group and directs the questions. Focus groups can be effective, especially when dealing with a new product introduction.

Focus groups can foster a feeling of friendship, even if it is only amongst a very small group of participants. People are usually flattered to be asked to participate. It makes them feel special to know that their opinions are so valued.

However, focus groups do have their problems. Since these groups are fairly small (often no more than twelve participants at a time), they really account for a very small segment of the buying population. The moderator must be well trained so that everyone in the group participates. You also have to be on the lookout for a dominant person who sways the opinions of others within the group. And finally, people are not always as candid as you would like them to be. They're trying to figure out what you want them to say, rather than what they really think.

5. Listening at the Higher Levels

Why don't companies pay more attention to their customers? It starts at the top. When management gets out of touch, the brand falters. It's not enough for senior level executives to attend an occasional focus group. Most of the time, the attitudes and behaviors of employees are really a reflection of management priorities. Management has to be willing to listen to employees as well as customers. Sam Walton, founder of Wal-Mart, once said, "The key to success is to get out into the store and listen to what the associates have to say. It's terribly important for everyone to get involved. Our best ideas come from clerks and stockboys."

If management sincerely believes that prospects and customers are important and deserve respect—and communicates this belief to everyone in the company—employees will treat customers with consideration and respect.

It's important that the highest level officers—the chairman, president, CEO, whatever the title—listen to real customers making real comments and complaints. That's what New Pig's Executive Vice President Doug Hershey does.

"The company has developed a customer problem database," he says. "When an employee deals with a customer complaint over the phone, he's required to put that complaint into the system. Those messages then go to several people throughout the company. So I'm seeing customer complaints whenever they occur. If somebody returns a product they're not happy with, I know about it. If somebody receives a package that was damaged in shipping, I know about it, and so do the other executives of the company. We are constantly in touch with what customers are saying; that way we know what needs to be fixed."

Company executives should themselves call and complain to find out exactly how complainers are treated.

The new paradigm is to be customer focused at all times. Find ways to communicate with customers, and then act on what they tell you. You have to listen to every single customer, because each one represents hundreds more who might be silent defectors.

Don't let them go without calling or writing to say, "I was just thinking about you." After all, that's what a friend would do!

Chapter Summary

- There are three major advantages to listening to all your customers:

    1. Listening makes people feel special and cared about.
    2. Listening alerts you to problems or opportunities that you didn't know existed.
    3. Listening builds relationships and develops rapport, trust, and understanding.

- The golden rule of Friendship Branding is to listen to your customers. They will tell you what they like about your product and, more important, what they don't like.

- What happens when you don't listen to your customers? You keep doing the same things over again, expecting different results.

- Following are five effective methods of keeping customer communications open:

    1. Database analysis
    Build new customer lists.
    Segment your customer list.
    Know when and why people stop being your customers.
    Watch out for silent defectors.

   2. Surveys
      Internet
      Direct mail
   3. Outbound telemarketing
   4. Focus groups
   5. High-level listening

- Remain customer focused at all times. Listen to every single customer, because each one represents hundreds more who might be silent defectors.

One of the surest evidences of friendship that one individual can display to another is telling him gently of a fault. If any other can excel it, it is listening to such a disclosure with gratitude, and amending the error.

—Baron Edward Lytton

Chapter Nine

Stage Five: Sharing with Your Customers

What Should Customers Know?

Bear with me, I'm going to say it again: If you want to keep your customers, you have to treat them as friends.

If you were moving, would you tell your friends? Of course.

If you were having financial problems, would you tell your friends? If they really were your friends, of course.

If you were planning a big change in your life, would you tell your friends? Well, what are friends for?

If you accomplished something you were proud of, would you tell your friends? Naturally.

If you knew you were about to disappoint your friends, for reasons beyond your control, or even if you'd made a mistake of some kind, would you tell them? Yes, because who would be more likely to forgive you?

That's the thing about friends—they share with each other what's important. They appreciate each other's good news and sympathize with each other's bad news. They are quick to feel pride in each other's achievements, to appreciate what they give each other, and to forgive each other their trespasses.

Everything I've just said applies to the buyer/seller relationship as well, or at least it can, when the buyer follows the principles of Friendship Branding. And when it does, it translates into that most desirable thing: a warm, emotional bond—and long-term loyalty.

Okay, let's get specific.

What can and should you tell customers about? Some things are obvious:

1. Tell them everything they could possibly need to know about their account or their current purchase. This includes quantity, size, color, price, shipping date, waybill number (if available), return information, etc.
2. Tell them where they can reach you if they have a question. Your phone number, mailing address, and e-mail address (if you have one, and you should) should be on *every* piece of paper you send to your customers. You're never shy about giving out your phone number when you want customers to order. Why not when you send a bill? When customers need to ask a question about your bill, nothing is more frustrating than not being able to find the phone number. Do you really think they'll get frustrated and

forget about the problem? The customers I know won't give up that easily and will only be angry with you for making communication difficult.

3. Tell them the name of the customer representative— the person who made the sale. The bigger the company, the more important this is. If you can personalize your company by putting a human face on it, you have significantly increased your chances of being seen as a friend. You've also given the customer someone specific to talk to, someone who understands his situation, empathizes with his problems, and is eager to keep him happy.

So much for the obvious. What about the less likely? What can you tell your best customers that is likely to help cement the relationship and win their loyalty?

Turns out, there's plenty.

The Good News

Everybody likes to have inside information. People love to be able to say, "I have a friend in the business." It's not just because they might be able to get a better price from an acquaintance; it's also because they like to be associated with "people in the know."

I discovered the value of this for myself with the Mason & Geller newsletter, "Inside Stuff." Four times a year, we let all our friends, colleagues, clients, and would-be clients know just what's been happening around our agency. We reported our move to larger offices in one of our newsletters (see Figure 9.1). I didn't want clients to think that just because we were

Inside Stuff

Vol.1 No.8 1998

The Mason & Geller Direct Marketing Newsletter

Greetings from Lois

Dear Friend:

It's a beautiful day and I'm sitting in my new office looking out on the New York City skyline writing to you with a touch of spring fever! I hope you're having a nice day, too.

When I was speaking at the Direct Marketing Days in Chicago, Barbara Dolan was at one of my sessions on "How to Add Personality to Your Direct Marketing." She was full of excitement about her new mail order business, Mail Order Bride. Her story was so interesting we're featuring her business in this issue.

We're also featuring Rebecca Smith's wonderful BagSmith Company in Cleveland. Her products are great, and I'm really hooked on the "Schlepper" bag she gave me!

I hope to hear from you about your DM challenges, opportunities and successes. So, please write or e-mail me. Everyone who writes gets one of my gifts as a thank you.

Please set up a visit to see us in our new offices. We can help with your DM programs. Also attend my seminar at Direct Marketing Days in New York on June 2nd, and on June 1st at the Women in Direct Marketing International Dinner.

All the best,

Lois

P.S. Please keep in touch with us. We love to hear from you!

I took Lois's advice and increased response by 35%!

by Rebecca Ruben Smith

It's amazing what a little well-timed advice can do! Last July, after reading RESPONSE!, I wrote to Lois.

We had developed a line of business and travel bags, marketed under the brand name of "The BagSmith." They're moderately priced, hip urban bags designed as an alternative to "outdoor-look" briefcases. Consumer marketing isn't our expertise, so we contacted agencies in Cleveland (our home base) asking for help. Here is a brief synopsis of their recommendations:

Agency A: Go on a four-day retreat to develop goals and strategic plan. Cost: $20,000.

Agency B: Ads in USAToday and the Wall Street Journal, two ads per week in each. Cost: $250,000

Agency C: A guerilla marketing approach, starting with broadcast faxes to test pricing and shipping issues. Cost: By project.

We chose Agency C and got immediate responses – from lawyers. Turns out broadcast faxes are against the law. That's when I wrote to Lois.

Lois advised that we try *New Yorker's* small advertisers program (4 ads for the price of 3). Figure A is the ad we ran in August. Lois told us that there wasn't enough benefit copy, and not enough "personality" in the ad. The bags looked nice, but there was nothing about the ad to really attract a reader's attention.

Lois's ideas resulted in a new headline just in time for the holidays: "O Come All Ye Schleppers." She also suggested adding the dimensions of the bags, and ideas about how to use them (e.g., "6 exterior pockets for umbrella, newspapers, gloves, cellular phone"). We got our own Christmas present when response jumped 35% over the previous ad!

We recently discovered that teachers love our tote bags, so we're running an ad in *Teacher Magazine* this month. Can't wait to see the results of this one!

Rebecca Ruben Smith can be reached at 1-888-879-7224 or by e-mail at **www.bagsmith.com.**

Figure A

Figure B
O Come, All Ye Schleppers-
Joyful and Triumphant!

Lois Geller's Speeches

May 12 , 1998 The President's Forum/Panelist NY Hilton - NYC 2:00pm/3:40pm	**August 11, 1998** Direct Marketing Association List Day Plaza Hotel - NYC 3:30pm
June 1, 1998 Women in Direct Marketing Dinner "The Great International Companies" NY Hilton - NYC 6:00pm	**September 17, 199** DMA Washington/ Central Virginia Richmond, VA 12:00pm
June 2, 1998 DMDNY-The How To's of Successful Direct Marketing NY Hilton - NYC 2:45pm	**October 12, 1998** DMA National Convention "Beyond Branding" Moscone Center, San Francisco, CA 1:00pm

Figure 9.1 Mason & Geller sends out its own newsletter four time as year to let clients and prospects know what's happening within the agency.

getting larger, they were going to lose touch with us. I reassured them that they were going to get the same personal service they had always gotten. We talk about people we hire, and we make announcements about people on our staff who want to share their own accomplishments (see Figure 9.2).

We also talk about our clients and what we're doing for them. Often another client will call and say, "I read the article about what you did for ABC Company. Can you do the same for me?" Our newsletter lets everyone know how we think and gives them a good idea of the tone and personality of our company.

That's why we call it "Inside Stuff." Everyone likes to know what goes on "inside" a brand. If you can tell a customer how a product is made, for instance, you can form a special bond with them. Several years ago, I was working on the account of a famous crystal company. We were marketing an unusual figurine that was actually difficult to produce. The ad we designed explained the process from beginning to end, and it was one of the best-selling items the company ever made. For the same reason, people love to visit the Hershey factory to see (and smell) the chocolates being made, or the Crayola plant to watch the familiar colored crayons being packed into their bright yellow boxes.

You can use any good news you have as an opportunity to keep your friendship going with your customers. Here are some examples:

If you're planning an expansion or you've decided to build new facilities, tell your best customers *before* the news makes the papers.

If you're bringing out a new product, tell your best customers as soon as you've made the decision.

Columbia House's New Welcome Package

Columbia House's new *play* positive option music club is attracting a lot of attention. You've probably seen their TV commercial with the two young men and the cute little dog and maybe you got their dramatic direct mail package. Columbia House is bound to bring in loads of new members and each and every one of them will receive their free CD's with an envelope, letter and 16-page welcome book created by Mason & Geller's Mike McCormick and art director Curtis Thomas, ably assisted by AE Patricia Sheridan and Production Manager Rob Ring.

Mike and Curtis gave the package a compelling and fun new personality with cartoon characters created by Chicago illustrator Patty O'Friel.

Join the club, get all that wonderful music and special money-saving offers and then enjoy the new welcome package. It looks great.

Inside Stuff Staff

Publisher: Lois Geller
Editors: Sharyn Kolberg, Michael McCormick
Design: Pepper Huff
Coordination: Sharyn Kolberg, Lorena Vega
Graphics: Pepper Huff, Curtis Thomas
Inside Stuff is published by:
Mason & Geller, LLC
261 Madison Avenue, 18th Fl
New York, New York 10016
212.697.4477
Fax: 212.697.2919
loisgeller@masongeller.com

M&G's Brain Power Expands Again

Account Supervisor Julia Crislip, working for her M.S. in Direct Marketing at NYU, has won not one but two prestigious scholarships this year: DMDNY's scholarship through NYU and the Silver Apple Scholarship. **Way to go Julia.**

Executive Assistant, Lorena Vega, earned her BA from William Paterson University in Wayne, NJ. **Outstanding!**

▲ Julia with Lois
◄ Lorena

Figure 9.2 To help clients put a "human" face on the Mason & Geller agency, the newsletter reports achievements of some of the staff.

If you've had a really good year, tell your best customers. And it wouldn't hurt to share a bit of the bounty with them, with a private sale, for instance.

If you're going to cut prices, tell your best customers first.

If you're adding to your staff, tell your best customers.

Every bit of good news that your best customers hear in advance of the general public will make them feel like part of the family, part of the in-group, in the know. It will tighten the bond they have with you and your company.

The Bad News

What should you tell your customers when the news is bad? Do you tell your good customers if you're discontinuing products they might like? Or if you're raising prices? Or if you've had a bad year? Do you tell them if you're laying people off? Or closing a facility?

Do you tell your good customers if you've been bought out? Do you tell them about product safety problems even if the government doesn't require it? Do you tell them if a senior executive—or perhaps their long-time customer representative—is leaving?

The answer in all cases is yes, absolutely. And you tell them before they have a chance to hear about it elsewhere. You tell them pre-emptively. And you tell them *your* way—not just the harsh truth but the harsh truth with an honest explanation and reasonable hope for recovery. You show respect for *their* needs and concerns, not just yours. You treat them like friends. And when friends need to know something about you, you don't withhold the information.

Think of how McNeil Consumer Healthcare handled the Tylenol poisonings a few years ago. The company president was absolutely upfront with consumers. He hid nothing. He pulled the entire product stock from store shelves, nationwide. Maybe that avoided lawsuits, but it didn't seem to be the reason he was doing it. He appeared to be taking that drastic action to protect his customers.

At the time, this was seen as an enormous risk. The company stock price plummeted. Both Wall Street and Madison Avenue were convinced Tylenol could never recover, that its day was done. And yet, that did not happen. Months later, Tylenol was back on the market. Soon afterward, it had regained its former market share.

Why? Because McNeil had practiced Friendship Branding. As important to them as the sale was, it wasn't as important as the customer.

The Tylenol brand could have been destroyed if McNeil acted differently—if, for instance, the company had stonewalled, or refused to recall its products, or otherwise tried to hide or diminish the problem.

Friendship Branding is not a pose. It is not a tactic. It is real. And it is an expression of something deeper than simple good business—although it is almost always good business as well. Friendship Branding is the expression of our concern and respect for each other. If we use the trappings of Friendship Branding to manipulate customers into believing we're the good guys, we denigrate the very idea of friendship.

I realize it is not traditional to talk of genuine human emotions in a business book, and maybe it's even a little startling. But we're embarking on a new millennium in which the old formulation—specifically "take the money and run"—

is no longer good business (if it ever was). It is an age in which buyers and sellers are partners in a transaction that can and should make winners out of both of them.

When You Make a Mistake: The "OOPS!" Letter

Most bad news that brands encounter is not life threatening, like the Tylenol scare or the tobacco industry's deceptions. It can be "brand threatening," however, as with the New Coke fiasco.

Several years ago, some hotshot at Coca-Cola decided that it was time to change the incredibly successful and well-loved formula for Coke. The company introduced New Coke, and it almost brought the whole brand down. The problem was that no one liked New Coke. Everyone loved Coke the way it was. Instead of insisting it was right, the company admitted it had made a mistake. It installed phone numbers for people to call in and vote for which Coke they preferred. Of course, Classic Coke won hands down, and they gradually phased New Coke off the market.

Anyone can make a mistake. Customers understand that. And they will almost always forgive you—as long as you admit the error of your ways. Years ago, when I was working for Ford of Canada, we sent out a mailing to both French- and English-speaking Quebec. The people of French-speaking Quebec get quite offended if you write to them in English. Unfortunately, the mailing we did got mixed up; the English letters went to the French-speaking people, and the French letters went to those who spoke English. As soon as we realized our mistake, we sent an "Oops!" letter of apology and offered people a free gift to come into their local Ford dealership. Not only did our customers accept our apology, but we got more sales from that program than from any we had done before. And I have written many an "Oops" letter since.

You can see one such letter in Figure 9.3. This "We're Sorry" letter was sent to apologize for a mistake in the company's billing procedures. Customers were supposed to receive a monthly bill for this series of videotapes, but the billing system was not working correctly, and the bills did not go out in a timely fashion. Because this was an error on the company's part, Mosby's offered customers a thirty-day deferred payment on the video they had ordered. Mosby's customers were more than happy to take advantage of that offer, and the company did not receive one complaint about the error.

In Friendship Branding, sellers tell buyers what they should know, what they need to know, and what they *deserve* to know. That doesn't mean they tell buyers *everything*. Buyers don't expect to hear about certain kinds of information—actual product or service costs, for instance. They probably don't expect to be told when two different brands really come off the same manufacturing line. They don't expect to be told your company is less efficient than your competitors.

They do expect, on the other hand, to buy your product or service at a fair price. They do expect it to work as promised. They do expect to be told about pertinent technical, legal, safety, and legislative issues.

In the 1970s, Herb Schmertz, the then vice president of public relations at Mobil Corporation, invented a way to tell people about Mobil's views on a variety of matters that affect the oil industry and its customers: He invented the Op-Ed column, so named because it consisted of a Mobil-written

Mosby

Dedicated to Publishing Excellence

Mosby–Year Book, Inc.
11830 Westline Industrial Drive
St. Louis, MO 63146
314 872 8370
800 325 4177
FAX 314 432 1380

WE'RE SORRY!

Dear Colleague,

We've already heard from so many nurses about how useful they found the first video of the *Pathophysiology for Nurses* series. They wanted to let us know how much they appreciate the outstanding visual quality and practical application of "Heart Failure and Pulmonary Edema." I hope you've had a chance to view your video, and that you agree with your colleagues. You may have already received the second video, "Coronary Artery Disease and Angina Pectoris." (If not, it's on its way).

We do, however, have to admit to a problem. You may not have received a bill for your videos. I apologize if this has caused you any inconvenience.

You'll find a new statement of your account enclosed with this letter. It will give you four important pieces of information:

- The video that was shipped most recently, and the balance due on it.
- Payments due on any previous orders.
- Payments previously received from you. (Payments mailed within the last five days will not show up on the statement).
- Total payment due on any current and/or past balance.

When we offered you this video series, we promised a no-risk preview period. So if you've received the first and second videos and haven't paid for either, you may choose to pay for one now and arrange for a 30-day deferred payment for the second. To do that, please call a Mosby service representative at 1-800-453-4351. And if you need to discuss any other aspect of your account, we'll be glad to help you with that, too.

Thank you for your patience. We value you as a customer, and want to have you in the Mosby family for many more years.

Sincerely,

Cindy Tryniszewski, RN, MSN
Clinical Director

Figure 9.3 This "Oops" letter sent to Mosby customers was an effective apology. The company received no complaints about the billing mistakes.

column on the page opposite to a newspapers' editorials (it appeared first in the *New York Times* and later in many other papers).

This column accomplished a number of Mobil goals. First, it drummed up support for its ideas on regulation, taxation, and similar questions. Second, it differentiated Mobil from the other major oil companies. They were silent; Mobil was outspoken. Third, and maybe most important, it gave Mobil an identity, a personality with whom customers could identify. It laid the basis for a warm emotional bond.

Friends Deserve to Know What's Going On

Why do companies keep things from their customers? Because they think of their customers not as friends but as *prey*. Their customers, while they might not put that in words, sense the attitude . . . and decide to become someone else's customers.

How can companies fix that attitude? Here's an example:

Imagine that you order an item from a catalog. For two weeks you receive nothing at all. Finally, you get a postcard saying the item is back ordered—you can wait to receive it, or you can cancel your order.

Now imagine that you order an item from another catalog. Two days later, you get a *phone call* from a company representative who says that your order arrived just after the stock had been exhausted. She tells you when new stock will be in and suggests similar items that can be shipped immediately. She also offers you the option of a cash refund.

Which of these companies would you order from again? Would you order again from the one that treated you like a friend, that gave you the information you needed in order to make an intelligent choice—or the one that told you the minimum that the law allows and treated you like one of the cattle in the process?

We all know the answer to that question. And yet, the vast majority of sellers—either of goods or services—communicate with their customers on a need to know basis. This may be fine in the CIA, but it doesn't sit well with the people who are providing you with a living—your customers, that is.

Driving Customers Away

My experience is that banks, in general, do a poor job of recognizing and servicing their best customers. My bank redid the branch where I usually go . . . and guess what? They got rid of the preferred customer line. So even if you have a balance of $10,000, you need to wait in the long line, *with everyone else*. They also replaced the spacious oak tables (where they keep deposit slips, etc.) with these narrow little check-writing tables. It's impossible to fill in a deposit slip and balance your pocketbook or attaché case on them! And wouldn't it be nice to think about adding tellers during peak hours? Well instead of adding another teller, there is a bank officer who queries the line asking if anyone needs help using the automated teller/deposit machine. I don't like that bank anymore!

I think the only reason more people don't change banks is that we get "hooked" in with our automatic deposit, automatic payments, and credit cards. In my mind, there is a great opportunity here for a bank that commits itself to really focusing on customer needs . . . and treating customers well.

In addition to not treating their customers well, it seems that banks hardly even recognize them—let alone reward them. I can't tell you how many times I've received an offer to open an account or get a credit card with a bank that I already have an account with. What's really disturbing is that they make these great offers to people they want as customers, and they don't offer anything to current customers. For example, I received a letter offering me a free safe deposit box for 1 year if I open an account at a particular bank. Well, I already have an account at this bank. When I brought the letter in to my branch and asked if I could get a free safe deposit box, the manager said no . . . that is only available to "new" customers.

Let Your Customers Know Who You Are

A while back, I placed an order with the Internet company eToys. Shortly thereafter, I received a letter from Toby Lenk, president of eToys. Now, while eToys is no longer in business, that letter illustrates a lot of what I've been saying about customer communication.

"Thanks for having shopped at eToys," he begins. "I just wanted to send a short note to tell you a little more about us and to show you how much we've grown in the past few months."

The letter went on to explain how Lenk got the idea for eToys—he was in a large toy store, couldn't find the gift he wanted for his niece, and couldn't find anyone to help him choose another. I could definitely relate to this experience, because I've had the same thing happen to me.

The letter continued on, in very simple, down-to-earth language, to tell me about all the different toys and games

I could find at eToys and urged me to look over the enclosed brochure. I was more than happy to look at the brochure; he sounded like a very nice fellow.

There was a P.S. to the letter: "If you have any comments or suggestions, send them directly to me at *tobylenk@etoys.com*. Although I can't respond to all of them, I'd love to hear what you have to say." I felt complimented and reassured by this, even though I didn't have anything to say at the time.

Then there was the finishing touch: A photo of Toby Lenk—not the grown-up Toby Lenk but the founder and CEO of eToys as he was at age four. He was a cute kid.

By the time I finished the letter and looked at the brochure, I was feeling a warm emotional bond toward eToys. I was ready to be friends. That's customer communication at its very best. And that's Friendship Branding.

Here's another example: Lands' End, the catalog company, knew that it had to put its catalog online. Concerned about the isolation of online shopping, the company figured out two different ways to improve communication with its customers. I spoke with Bill Bass, Lands' End's vice president of e-commerce and he outlined how the company was trying to overcome this obstacle:

Method one: "Lands' End Live." This system allows customers to send an e-mail to customer service requesting the help of a personal assistant as they browse the site. The customer looks at the pages while asking the personal shopper questions about size, color, price, availability, or fabrics, for instance. The assistant can also help mix and match outfits and answer questions. This can be done through an "instant chat" feature on the company's Web site or by telephone, with both customer and assistant talking while they view the same Web pages.

Method two: "Shop with a Friend." This method allows two friends in separate locations to browse on the same page while comparing prices and exchanging opinions over instant chat.

"We asked ourselves, 'What are some of the perks of shopping in a store that we don't have online yet?' Shopping can be a very social experience. So we decided to offer customers the option of shopping with a friend or a salesperson."

This is an excellent example of Friendship Branding, because the company involved, Lands' End, truly empathized with its customers and responded to their needs. At the same time, it established new and very personal channels of communication. It went beyond the usual catalog descriptions of an item to offer an online personal assistant who could actually discuss items with the customer.

And something else was going on here too, something very subtle. In instant chats everywhere, the people typing to each other tend very quickly to bond, to become friends, even to become emotionally involved. Was Lands' End thinking that this same phenomenon would happen between its customers and its online personal assistants? Maybe so, maybe not. But I can think of no better way to build the emotional bond that leads to long-time customer loyalty.

The lesson here is that whenever you provide customers with information, you should personalize it. Don't simply call your customers by name; name yourself as well. Communication should never come from "The Institution" to "The Customer." It should come from Toby Lenk, CEO (or Amy

Brown, personal assistant; or Dan Church, credit manager; or Bill Stevens, service manager), to Lois Geller, customer.

After all, companies are only collections of people. So if you want to build the emotional bond between your customers and your company, put your customers in touch with your people every time you have the chance. Let them make friends.

Communicating on a "Need to Know" Basis

One evening, not long ago, I was sitting in a crowded airplane out at the edge of the runway. I guess the engines were running, but it was hot in the plane nonetheless.

The cabin lights were low, and the reading lights were off. I couldn't see much out the windows—the sun had already set. The flight attendants, I suppose, were sitting in their seats. At any rate, they weren't circulating through the cabin.

I assumed that we were just waiting in a take-off line and that we'd soon be airborne. So I tried to be patient (not an easy task in my case). Usually, when you're waiting in a take-off line, your plane advances every so often as the line shortens. That didn't happen this time. We just sat there.

After about twenty minutes, you begin to wonder. After an hour, steam begins to shoot out of your ears. You want to know what's going on. You are starved for information. Even the phrase "won't be long now" would be a Godsend.

But on this occasion, nothing.

Then, suddenly, the passenger door opened. A mechanic hoisted himself into the plane, then reached down and lifted a huge box inside, which he proceeded to drag into the cockpit.

Still no word from anyone. No flight attendant fluttering through the aisles, reassuring us. No pilot on the loudspeaker. Just silence. Do they let pilots fly with laryngitis?

After about twenty minutes more, the scene with the mechanic played backward and he shut the cabin door behind him. Another twenty minutes passed. We were fast coming up to two hours on the runway without a word from any employee of the airline.

Suddenly, the second engine started up. The cabin began to cool. We rolled forward, and, a few minutes later, took off. At that point, the flight attendants emerged from wherever they'd been hiding.

"What was that delay all about?" half a dozen passengers asked simultaneously.

Whatever the problem was, keeping your mouth shut isn't the way you'd deal with your friends and it isn't the way a company should deal with its customers, not if it wants to keep them, not if it finds the notion of Friendship Branding a persuasive one. Smart companies treat their customers like insiders, like part of the family, like friends who deserve to know the truth—whatever it is—and aren't likely to take advantage of their knowledge.

Chapter Summary

- You should share this information with your customers:

    Everything possible about their account or current purchase
    Where they can reach you if they have a question
    The name of the customer representative who made the sale

- Make your customers feel like part of your family. Share your good news with them, especially if you're doing the following:

  Planning an expansion or building new facilities
  Bringing out a new product or product line
  Having a really good year
  Going to cut prices
  Adding to your staff

- Share the bad news as well, especially if you're doing the following:

  Planning to raise prices
  Discontinuing a product or product line
  Having a really bad year
  Closing a facility
  Having problems or have made a mistake

- Personalize all your communications. Every letter or e-mail should be signed by a particular person (not just with the company name).

Piglet sidled up behind Pooh. "Pooh," he whispered.
"Yes, piglet?"
"Nothing," said Piglet, taking Pooh's paw. "I just
wanted to be sure of you."

—*A. A. Milne*

Chapter Ten

Stage Six: Making Customers Feel Secure

Not long ago, I was shopping at a Neiman Marcus store in a huge suburban mall. I'd picked out a half-dozen assorted blouses, skirts, and slacks, adding up the prices in my head, until I reached my limit. Unfortunately, that came all too soon—none of the items were on sale.

I took my selections to a register, and the sales clerk began the checkout process, scanning the bar codes on the merchandise tags. I watched the register so that I could make sure I'd still have taxi money after I paid.

Suddenly, I noticed a discrepancy. A $40 dollar blouse rang up at $25. Then an $80 pair of slacks registered as $60. By the time the clerk was finished ringing me up, I was paying $100 less than I'd figured.

I was trying to rationalize a way to not tell the clerk she'd made a mistake when she spoke up.

"Oh, you're getting the sales price on those four items," she said pointing.

"I didn't know they were on sale."

"Well, the ad doesn't come out until Wednesday, but it's our policy to automatically give customers the sales price if they buy something the day before the sale starts."

"But it's two days before the sale starts."

The clerk smiled. "We don't like to take chances with our good customers," she said.

Now I wasn't really a good customer at Neiman's. I'd bought a few things there now and then, but I was mainly a Saks and Bloomingdale's person, until the moment that sales clerk charged me $100 less than I'd expected to pay.

Most of the stores I know would not have been as considerate as Neiman's was that day. Most of them would have kept quiet about special sales and gladly taken the full price. Many of them would have resisted mightily if you'd bought something on Monday at full price, seen the sales ad on Wednesday, and come in Thursday asking for an adjustment.

The object of Friendship Branding is to create a warm emotional bond between buyer and seller, and that's what Neiman Marcus did that day. I felt valued, I felt special, but, more than that, I felt I was dealing with an honorable company. I felt I could trust Neiman Marcus to look after my interests, not to take advantage of me, to treat me, well, as a friend would.

That's Friendship Branding at its best.

This summer, while on vacation, I rented a car from Hertz. Unfortunately, I managed to back it into a concrete post, cracking the back bumper and damaging the left rear panel.

When I nervously returned the car, the Hertz parking attendant glanced at the damaged rear end and told me to see the agent inside. I sheepishly approached the counter.

"I'm afraid I banged up your new car," I told the agent.

"I'm sorry to hear that," she said. "I hope it didn't ruin your vacation."

I don't know exactly what I'd expected from her—maybe a deep sigh, a rolling of the eyes, a stern reprimand ("That car was reserved by someone else for next week, you know,") and a clear statement of my liability ("You know you're going to have to cover all the damage, and we'll need your payment promptly,"), followed by getting my signature on a four-page form in triplicate that amounted to signing away my firstborn if I didn't meet my obligations.

Instead, she said, "I hope it didn't ruin your vacation."

"Actually, it wasn't a problem," I assured her. "The trunk still opens and closes, so I didn't have any problems getting to my luggage or locking it up."

"Well, don't worry about it. Things like that happen all the time. Your insurance will probably cover it, and if not, you used your American Express card and their insurance will take care of you. I'm glad you weren't inconvenienced."

She gave me a short form to fill out. I wrote a one-sentence description of the accident and signed the paper. "That should take care of it," the agent said with a smile. "We'll be in touch by mail."

I walked away from the counter like I'd been given an unexpected—and probably undeserved—reprieve.

To this day, I don't know if Hertz agents are trained to react to customer accidents that way, or if I was just lucky to get a warm and sympathetic agent. I hope it's part of Hertz's training, and National's, Budget's and everyone else's, because it's a fine example of Friendship Branding.

The Hertz agent worried first about me and my life, not about her company. She treated me the way a friend would. She recognized my discomfort and defused it. She treated me with respect.

Now, I have no intention of banging up another rental car, but I can tell you this: The next time I rent a car, you can be sure it will be a Hertz. I want to know that if anything goes wrong, I will be treated with care and consideration.

Treat Your Customers with Care and Compassion

I think that Friendship Branding requires one further step: up-front care and compassion. I'm only talking about an attitude adjustment. I believe companies should train their employees to look at inconvenienced customers as real people with real problems and treat them as *they* would like to be treated in similar circumstances. They should emphasize good will toward all—an old saying, maybe, but one that's still valid.

The idea here is to convince customers that someone knowledgeable is on their side and working hard to solve their problems, that the individual behind the counter is a human being, not just a computer operator, that they have a *friend* behind the counter. This approach will do more than just reassure displaced customers. It will change *their* attitude, from anger to acceptance, from helplessness to hopefulness. It will make life easier for the employees behind the counter. It will leave customers with the memory of someone sticking up for them when the going got tough. And that's more than halfway toward building a warm emotional bond.

Can this actually work? Well, I know it works in reverse. When I'm facing a delay or a cancellation at the airport and have to rely on the help and goodwill of a counter agent, I always start the conversation by saying, "It must be terrible for you when this happens—passengers making demands, passengers getting angry, passengers blaming you. I feel badly for you."

The result is always the same: a look of surprise, a genuine smile, and a dedicated effort to solve my transportation problems. How would passengers feel if the agents said something like this: "I understand how important that appointment is, and I'm going to do my absolute best to get you there on time," or "We're going to call your grandmother right now and tell her your flight will be delayed. We don't want her to wonder what's going on," or "I'm not sure we can get you home tonight, but if we can't, we're going to put you up in a beautiful hotel, pay for your meals, and get you a first-class seat on the first flight tomorrow."

Who could still be angry if the agent treated them with that kind of care and compassion? And who wouldn't have friendly feelings toward the airline despite the delay?

Unfortunately, few agents talk to passengers this way. Few sellers really try to put themselves in the buyer's shoes. Fewer still think of—or treat—their customers the way they treat their friends.

And it's not just the way companies talk to customers. It's also their behavior. Companies behave dishonorably toward their customers all the time, unfortunately. They make shoddy goods, overprice them, don't repair them when they break, won't make exchanges, and otherwise behave as if the only matter of importance between themselves and their customers is the money they can extract from them.

Outstanding Customer Service

Undoubtedly, the best way to be a Friendship Brander is to practice outstanding customer service. Following are some key elements to customer service.

Timely Delivery

One of the reasons I order from a particular Chinese restaurant in my neighborhood is because they deliver quickly. The food is no better (or worse) than several other restaurants in my area, but they make a point of getting it to me fast. And that's important when you're tired, hungry, and looking forward to a tasty meal.

You never want to disappoint your customers. If you do make deliveries, you have to be sure that they occur within the time you promise, or you must notify customers that you will be late and give them an option to cancel their order. Customers expect and deserve timely delivery. If they're ordering something they want or need and it takes too long to arrive, they may go out and buy it elsewhere (and return the one they got from you). A birthday or holiday present that arrives one day too late can easily cost you a customer.

No Hidden Charges

Customers want to be able to trust you. They don't want to have to be on the lookout for the fine print or for hidden charges. They want to know that you have their best interest at heart. Customers are truly disappointed when something they thought was a bargain turns out to be fairly expensive. One music club, for example, has been losing much of its customer base because it turns out that their offer of "12 CDs for 99¢" carries a hefty $30 delivery charge—which customers don't even find out about until they receive an invoice along with their delivery. That's not only not friendly, it's downright sneaky.

In an April 5, 1999, article in the *New York Times,* Bob Tedeschi reported that many Internet consumers were experiencing "clicker shock" when they found out, at the end of a sometimes long and involved ordering process, that the final selling price of a product could be as high as 40 percent more than the advertised price, once the shipping and handling were added. The article quoted Jakob Nielsen, who advises companies on how to make Web sites easier to use, as saying, "There's a danger of the web turning into a low-trust environment, and this adds to it. You feel like you've got to be on guard constantly, because people are trying to cheat you. You might still buy, but it's not a pleasant experience." And customers might buy from you once, but it's likely they'll look elsewhere next time.

One Geller Branding Survey recipient relates such an unpleasant experience with a catalog:

> I received a special price discount catalog from a major mail-order house. I called the day I received the catalog and attempted to order six different items. Five of them were sold out! I was thrilled that the sixth item was in stock, until they told me that shipping charges go by the weight of the item. As far as I was concerned, that made the "discount" null and void. I won't be ordering from them any time soon.

Flexibility

One of the most frustrating experiences a shopper can have is being told, "Sorry, that's our policy," or "There's nothing we can do about that." Customers want to be listened to by someone with a positive attitude who is willing to help them solve their problems.

For example, last spring my neighbor traveled to Italy. When he came back, there was a credit card bill waiting for him. He had missed the due date because of his trip. Even though my neighbor had been a customer for twenty-five years, the credit card company threatened to cancel the card immediately if they didn't receive payment. Friends don't threaten one another. Friends give friends a chance to make good on their debts. My neighbor canceled the card.

Give customers options whenever possible. For example, if possible, allow the customer to choose the best time of the month to pay his or her bill. Believe it or not, this is one area of Friendship Branding practiced by the IRS! If a taxpayer cannot pay a tax debt in one lump sum, he can call the agency and arrange to pay in installments. The IRS allows him to choose how much he will pay each month (within certain guidelines, of course) and on which day the payment will be due. This kind of accommodation goes a long way toward making customers feel secure within the business relationship.

If you're a purveyor of goods or services and something goes wrong, my best advice is to treat the customer at least fairly and, if possible, better than fairly. If there's ever a time to take the money and run, which I doubt, this isn't it. This is the time to treat your customer the way you'd like to be treated in the same circumstances.

Easy Return Policy

I believe that every merchant should have a money-back guarantee, especially if you are selling items via Direct Mail or the Internet, when customers can't see or touch the real thing until it's delivered. They should be given the opportunity to check it out at home. Customers need to know that if they make a mistake in ordering, or if they are not satisfied with the merchandise they receive, they have the option to change their minds. It should not be a difficult process. Many companies include preaddressed return labels so that customers know exactly how and where to return merchandise.

One company that has a true Friendship Branding return policy is the Lillian Vernon Corporation. Lillian Vernon was a pioneer in offering personalized merchandise by mail. In 1951, Vernon Specialties (as the company was then called) placed its first ad in *Seventeen Magazine,* offering purses and belts with a unique service—personalization with the customer's initials free of charge (see Figure 10.1).

Vernon believes that's one of the reasons she has such a loyal customer base. "Every product we sell has a 100% customer satisfaction, money-back guarantee," she says. "You can return any product for any reason, including those that have

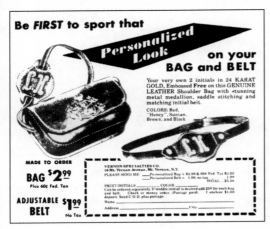

Figure 10.1
The $495 ad that launched the Lillian Vernon Corporation appeared in the September 1951 issue of *Seventeen Magazine.*

been personalized, even ten years after it is purchased. This policy was established when I started my company 49 years ago and has remained a company hallmark. I firmly believe that is why our customer database has grown to over 22 million people."

Another company with an outstanding return policy is Lands' End. They promise to knock themselves out for their customers (see Figure 10.2). They not only guarantee an

Figure 10.2 Lands' End makes their customers feel secure by promising (and delivering) customer service that goes above and beyond—and a 100 percent money-back guarantee. (Reprinted with permission of Lands' End, Inc.)

exchange or refund "any time, for any reason," but also offer to ship items within two business days, and to hem or cuff your pants for free. They have specialty shoppers to answer questions about sizing and claim to have phone people who are "simply the friendliest around." There couldn't be a better example of Friendship Branding!

When They Don't Like What They Buy

At both the retail and the wholesale level, seller policies vary widely when it comes to customer returns, but generally they fall into four groups:

1. You buy it; it's yours—or take the money and run. Some sellers live by this policy. Others apply it mainly to sales or closeout merchandise.
2. You give us money; you never get it back—or exchange yes; refund no. When products like video games are involved, the exchanges are limited to the same title, so buyers can't buy one, then keep exchanging it again and again until they've played with the complete stock.
3. You buy it; we'll give you a refund—if we can put it back in stock without refolding, repacking, or re-ticketing it. Clothing stores, which are very wary of one-night uses followed by full refunds, often have this policy.
4. You buy it; we'll give you a refund, no questions asked—doesn't matter if the item is used or broken or old. This is the total customer satisfaction policy, which can be found at stores like L. L. Bean and some catalog operations.

Now which of these meets the criteria for Friendship Branding? Which is the way a friend would treat another friend? In my opinion, it's no. 4.

Of course, if you're willing to give out refunds for any reason at any time, a small percentage of people will take advantage of you, and that's true of friends as well. But the other 95 percent will feel like you really care about them, that there's more to the relationship than the simple exchange of money for goods or services.

In the direct marketing industry, studies have shown that fewer than 5 percent of shipments are returned (although this figure is slightly higher for clothing items). People who do return items will long remember that you didn't hassle them when they asked for a refund, that they didn't have to come up with some kind of possibly bogus reason, and that you didn't keep their money and force them to buy something else. Customers who are given an instant refund, complete with a smile, when they feel the need to return merchandise they've purchased from you, will feel that they've been treated like the honorable people they are. As a result, you can feel reasonably sure they'll be back. They'll buy more. And the next time, they'll probably *keep* what they've bought. All this because they'll feel that warm emotional bond that inspires customer loyalty.

Yes, this policy costs a bit. But it brings with it the reward of a legion of loyal customers, paying for itself many times over.

If It's Broken When They Receive It

So far, I've been talking about merchandise being returned not because it was damaged or needed repair but because it simply wasn't what the customer wanted for one reason or another.

Now, let's consider merchandise that arrived broken, or doesn't work, or needs repair. If you want loyal customers, and I assume you're reading this book because that's one of your goals, the principles of Friendship Branding require you to handle customer repair problems promptly, completely, and with a minimum of fuss and formality.

A few years ago, someone gave me a sterling silver Cross pen. I loved the way it looked, the way it felt in my hand, and how it wrote. I used it all the time. Occasionally, I dropped it. Since silver is a relatively soft metal, the pen barrel got slightly dented each time it hit the floor. Soon, my beautiful Cross pen wasn't so beautiful any more.

So I looked up the company address, packaged up the pen, put in a note asking them to replace the barrel and send me a bill, and mailed it off. Less than ten days later, I received a gleaming new sterling silver Cross pen in the mail. Enclosed with it was a small card that said all Cross products are guaranteed for life. There was no charge.

I still have that Cross pen. I've been very careful with it, so it's free of dents. And almost every time I look at it, I remember that Cross once replaced it, free. Do I have that warm emotional bond with Cross? You bet I do.

To be sure, repairs are sometimes limited by the length of warrantees. But my advice is to be as generous as possible, even when the item comes in after the warrantee has expired. I know that car manufacturers frequently offer free repairs after the warrantee period has expired, especially if there's any suspicion that it just took a long time for a defect to show up. That kind of policy makes friends and wins customer loyalty.

Friendly Debt Collection

For many companies—credit card issuers, department stores, gasoline providers—when a customer is late with a payment, he ceases to be a customer. He becomes a debtor. I believe this is a serious mistake. It's a major opportunity lost.

Dozens of different studies show that once people become customers, they tend to *stay* customers. They become repeat customers. They buy the product or the service again and again. What's more, they don't need to be wooed with the same amount of energy it takes to land new customers.

The people who owe you money—even when they're late—are still customers. Some, it's true, may be deadbeats, either on purpose or through circumstances beyond their control. But the vast majority will straighten out their financial problems and be able to buy again. Wouldn't you like them to buy from you?

All this is why, when debt collecting, companies should never forget they're talking not so much to debtors but to once and future customers. They should treat these folks with respect and compassion. They should avoid humiliating them, angering them, or otherwise mistreating them. They should act toward them exactly the way they would act toward friends; they should assume they are honorable and give them the benefit of the doubt.

For some small percentage of people, that will be better treatment than they deserve. But for all the rest, it will inspire gratitude and loyalty. It will reinforce the warm emotional bond that is at the heart of successful Friendship Branding.

Don't Practice Threatening Debt Collection

Here's an example of how *not* to treat your customers:

One of my relatives, a thirty-ish family man, is a nice, well-intentioned fellow, but he tends to get in over his head, financially speaking. We'll call him George—not his real name, but he knows who he is.

Anyhow, George is a bit too reliant on plastic. He has four or five major credit cards, in addition to the everyday living expenses for himself and his family. Sometimes, he gets behind. And when he's behind, the telephone starts ringing . . . and ringing . . . at all hours.

George is an honest fellow, and he always pays his bills, eventually. But until he does, he often has to talk to bill collectors. He tells me they have several approaches:

- *They provide a "double whammy."* "Someone will call and tell me how much I owe and when it's due. He'll ask when I can pay, and he'll say that he's making a note on my account. Then he hangs up. A week later, another person calls (well before the agreed-upon payment date), and I have the identical conversation with him."
- *They demand explanations.* "They want to know why I'm late. They kind of force me to make up stories. You know, like I had to get the furnace repaired or I had to go to the dentist or something similar. Sometimes they ask questions, but mostly they just listen and write it down. I can usually come up with a good story for them, although sometimes I wonder what they'd say if I simply told them I'd spent too much."

- *They warn you of the consequences.* "If you get behind another month," they say, "we'll have to report it to the credit bureau. You wouldn't want that, because it could affect your credit. And that could hurt your career opportunities and have many other unpleasant effects."

- *They threaten.* They say things like, "We expect your payment within twenty-four hours. Remember, you signed a contract with us. If we don't hear from you promptly, the entire amount will be due and payable immediately. We'll turn the bill over to a collection agency. We'll sue. We won't rest until we get the entire amount due us. We'll call every other day until you satisfy your debt. You gave us your *word* you'd pay. What is your word worth?"

- *They comfort.* "Everyone gets behind now and then," they say. "I understand. I've been late a few times myself. We know you want to pay, but you just can't right now. How about if we put you on a plan that lowers payments, lowers interest, cancels late and over-limit payments for a few months? Will that solve the problem?"

- *They propose solutions.* "Have you considered having a yard sale? How about getting a home equity loan? Have you spoken with a credit counseling agency? Maybe you can get a loan from friends or relatives. Perhaps you could get along without *two* cars."

If bill collectors are not calling people, they're sending threatening letters, like the one below (this is an actual collection letter; the company names have been changed to avoid them coming after me!):

YOU FAILED TO COMPLY

THIS IS ANOTHER REQUEST FROM ACME COLLECTION COR-PORATION THAT YOU SETTLE THIS OVERDUE BALANCE OF **$14.70.**

YOU FAILED TO RESPOND TO PREVIOUS PAYMENT DEMANDS AND WE BELIEVE THAT YOU MAY BE ATTEMPTING TO AVOID THIS JUST DEBT. YOU NEED TO CHANGE OUR MINDS AS QUICKLY AS POSSIBLE.

IT IS IMPORTANT TO UNDERSTAND THAT XYZ CORPORA-TION HAS GIVEN THIS COLLECTION AGENCY THE RESPON-SIBILITY TO COLLECT THE **$14.70** YOU OWE. ACME COLLECTION CORPORATION IS PREPARED TO TAKE ADDI-TIONAL COLLECTION MEASURES, IF NECESSARY, TO RESOLVE THIS MATTER.

NOTE: *THIS ACCOUNT HAS BEEN ADDED TO THIS AGENCY'S DELINQUENT FILE.*

DO NOT IGNORE THIS IMPORTANT MESSAGE. *SEND YOUR PAYMENT TODAY!*

Imagine all this fuss over $14.70! It must have cost the company more than that to collect this debt. And all it did was make this customer angry.

When companies, especially those that have promised friendship and customer service, use this frightening tone, what happens to their warm and fuzzy image? A gentler approach might be more effective (especially with such a small amount): "We have not yet received payment from you for the amount shown on the enclosed invoice. Please take a moment to check your records. If you have already sent in your payment, we would like to thank you. If you have not, please note that your payment is expected within ten days."

"I respond best to the people who treat me well," says George. "People who have sympathy for me, who don't try to make me feel like a ne'er-do-well, a spendthrift, or a lazy bum, the people who treat me like a person, not a bank account, the people who don't assume I'm dishonest. I try to pay them *something,* and I try to pay as soon as I can."

"The people who get paid last are the intimidators, the ones who act as though I've committed some kind of sin, like I'm some kind of moral leper. Those people seem to take pleasure in making me feel worse than I already do, and they assume I'm intent on ripping them off. When the money finally starts coming in and I start paying off my bills, these are the ones I pay last. In fact, I stop doing business with these outfits."

Show Your Appreciation

To begin with, the moment after a sale is closed is the right time to say "thanks." I know everyone says it, from the shoeshine guy to the car salesman. But ninety-nine times out of a hundred, that "thank you" is perfunctory at best. It's part of the routine. It's reflexive.

I suggest that it be elevated into something genuine. What I'm talking about is recognizing, at least implicitly, that the two of you, the customer and the seller, just did something good. That could consist of a firm handshake, significant eye contact, and a statement of appreciation that doesn't sound like it comes from a sales training manual. Or it could consist of a handwritten note and maybe an invitation to a company event of some sort. The object is to build the relationship, to take definite steps toward creating that warm emotional bond that leads to loyalty.

Imagine this: You buy a new car, a BMW, for instance. The salesperson says all the right things at the moment the sale is made. But then she does something more. A few days later you receive a beautiful key chain from Tiffany & Co. for your new car keys.

Or imagine this: You purchase a computer from, say, Dell. The entire transaction takes place on the Internet. You fill in forms, click on some options, fill in your credit card information, and, a few days later, boxes arrive on your doorstep.

Two days later, you get a call from Dell. The "customer representative," as he calls himself, asks you if you've had any problems with the setup and offers to talk you though it if you haven't started. Then he asks you how you'll be using the machine. If you say, "It's a family machine," he says, "Good. I have some games I'm going to send you." If you say it's for work, he says, "Good. I have some great Internet utilities I'm going to send you."

And every six months or so after that, he calls again to discuss how the machine has been working and to solve any problems you may be having, and he sends you something more—free.

Three years later, you're ready for a new machine. "I think I'll call that customer representative at Dell," you tell yourself. "I'm sure he'll be able to take care of me." That's Friendship Branding at its best.

Friendship Branding isn't easy for big companies. They can say and do all the right things and still come off as impersonal. IBM used Charlie Chaplin in one famous series of TV commercials, and maybe that made us smile; but we still had a hard time equating the IBM monolith with the little tramp.

So what's a big company to do? Here's one suggestion:

Assign permanent representatives to your best customers—one person who can handle every aspect of the relationship from sales through service. That person can serve as the permanent liaison between the customer and other parts of the organization.

This way, the company would always speak with a single voice, and the customer would never be shuttled from department to department, having to repeat her story each time. It would provide the consistency and knowledge needed to build a good relationship.

If they have enough resources, well-organized companies could apply this technique to all customer contacts. Here's how it would work:

Let's say you call a company. You're seeking information, or help, or you want to buy something, or you need to return something, or you want to check a price. The person who answers your telephone is the customer representative. He or she is your guardian angel, at least for this call. Whatever your problem or question, this guardian angel stays with you—on the phone—until you're taken care of. If the guardian angel can handle it all alone, fine. But if others must be contacted or called, it's the guardian angel who does the calling—while you stay on the phone. And he doesn't say goodbye until you are completely satisfied.

In this system, you're never told to call another number. You are never transferred. You're never put on hold for more than a minute. You're never forced to tell your story or make your request a second time. You are treated with respect, kindness, and friendliness by one single human being.

The purpose of all this is to show the customer—and not just tell her—that she matters to you, that the relationship is more important than the sale, that you are ready, willing, and able to take care of her needs and questions.

And the effect of this demonstration is to help form that warm emotional bond that leads to customer loyalty. The size of your company doesn't matter at all. Anyone can practice Friendship Branding and create loyal customers. Here are two reports from respondents to the Geller Branding Survey in which that's exactly what happened. The first respondent tells the story of a flight he took with British Airways:

> During my flight to England, my old suitcase fell apart in cargo. They automatically replaced it with a brand-new suitcase without asking any questions. They were incredibly nice throughout my dealings with them, and I wouldn't hesitate to fly with them again.

The second respondent had a surprising experience with her Illuminations catalog customer service:

> I ordered merchandise from their catalog. One of the items consisted of three glass pieces in a set. Upon opening the box, I cracked one of the glass pieces. I called their "800" number and explained the fact that I had broken the glass myself. The operator insisted that

they replace the item free of charge. I was doubly delighted when I received the package and discovered that they had replaced the complete set—all three pieces—at no charge.

Show Your Customers You Value the Relationship More Than the Sale

News bulletin: Money is the glue between buyer and seller. That's cold and crass, perhaps, but it's the truth, and we all know it. Obvious as it is, though, it is not the *whole* truth, and we often lose sight of that.

There is a moment, if we pause long enough to notice it, when something distinctly nonmonetary takes place between buyer and seller, something *emotional*. Somewhere, probably in his subconscious, the seller takes pleasure from the implied approval he's getting from the buyer. He takes pleasure in knowing that he's pleased the buyer and that he's had the skill—or been likeable enough—to close the sale.

The buyer has the mirror image of that emotional moment. His purchase gives him pleasure, even when he's purchased a practical item like a hammer. He's pleased that he has the resources to do the deal. He's pleased that one of his needs or desires have been filled.

At this moment, buyer and seller are partners. Maybe they were a bit adversarial during the sales process, but now they're pals. They've done something good—together.

Unfortunately, this moment is little noted and rarely celebrated. It's allowed to fade away to nothing so that the next time buyer and seller meet on the field of transactions, they have to start from scratch, relationshipwise.

The principles of Friendship Branding call for a different outcome, one that extends and expands the magical moment just following the sale. It calls for the buyer, at least, to recognize the opportunity to build something that goes beyond the cash register.

Don't Come on with a Rush, Then Disappear

Many sellers of goods or services are like suitors. They're spectacular at courtship, but when it comes to the marriage part, they're barely adequate, if that. These companies are absolutely wonderful at getting new customers. They offer a cornucopia of special deals, special rates, special service, and, generally, special treatment.

But as soon as the seduction is complete, they don't seem to care. The customer never hears from them again, except if he accidentally stumbles over one of those new customer offers that company is making again.

This is not Friendship Branding. It's not good business either, since all the studies show continuing customers are far more valuable, over time, than a decade's worth of new customers.

So what's a company to do?

Well, you might as well ask what's a suitor to do, once the marriage is made. The short answer: Never stop courting. Keep those flowers, boxes of chocolate, and little gifts coming.

If you keep up the courtship, you greatly improve your chances of holding onto that new customer. Consider it relationship maintenance.

If you're a suitor, there are a thousand different ways to keep up the courtship, ways that will last until you're both old and gray. But if the relationship is a commercial one, you'll need some imagination and a lot of persistence.

Here are some Friendship Branding ideas that can maintain that relationship between buyer and seller:

- *Private sales.* Imagine how you'd respond if a Macy's representative called you out of the blue and invited you to a "best customers" private, after-hours sale.
- *Special events.* "We're having a special showing of the Hottest New Movie at the Bijou Theater on Sunday afternoon and we're inviting our best customers. Even the popcorn is free."
- *Special treatment.* "Gold card customers have a special sales desk—no need to wait in line for a cashier. We'll check you out while you have a cup of coffee, on us."
- *Personal shoppers.* "Best customers get a personal shopper, who keeps track of your needs, makes sure you never run out of supplies, and alerts you to special deals that might interest you."
- *Information and education.* Stonyfield Farm is not your average yogurt company. They are "150 people in a small New Hampshire town who are committed to producing the best-tasting, healthiest yogurts, frozen yogurts, and ice cream possible." Part of their mission is to educate consumers about yogurt, and about the environment. Recently, an offer printed on the underside of the yogurt lid invited customers to send away for a free booklet that talked about the health benefits of eating yogurt (see Figures 10.3 and 10.4). This is a great way to make friends with your customers. And

Samuel Kaymen with his grandkids

Stonyfield Farm Founder and Chairman, Samuel
Kaymen with grandkids, Ian and Alysa Lewandowski

Special Thanks To:

Joanne Curran Celentano, Ph.D.
Food and Nutritional Sciences, professor at the
University of New Hampshire, and long-time
Stonyfield Farm yogurt eater, for answering our
customers' nutrition questions.

Brooke Vinstein, MBA
Stonyfield Farm devotee, and proponent of
socially responsible business, for volunteering
her time and talent to work on this brochure.

Figure 10.3 To let customers
know they "want you to feel
good inside," and to educate
them about the health benefits
of eating yogurt, Stonyfield
Farms offers customers this
free booklet.

Figure 10.4 Stonyfield Farm
encourages customers to feel
like part of their family by
including this photograph of
Samuel Kaymen (founder and
chairman) and his grandchildren.

on the stonyfield.com Web site, visitors can participate in the "Have-A-Cow Educational Program," which allows them to "adopt" a Stonyfield cow. Participants receive a photograph of their cow, her biography, and information about life on a modern-day farm. What better way to make customers feel that they are part of the Stonyfield family!

All of the preceding information, in fact, everything in this chapter, has a single purpose: to convince your customers that they can count on you, to make them feel that when they deal with you, they are secure, and they don't have to worry.

This is a crucial part of friendship and a crucial part of Friendship Branding. As Dom Rossi, publisher of *Reader's Digest,* says, "One of the things that makes *Reader's Digest* a great brand is that it has established a relationship with consumers that is built on a great sense of credibility and trust. In many respects, it is an oasis in the onslaught of media alternatives. People escape with *Reader's Digest* . . . we maintain friendships with our customers because we hear them when they say, 'Understand me, be honest with me, be there for me, and whatever you do—don't disappoint me!'"

Chapter Summary

- Never lose sight of care and compassion. Even bill collecting can be done with a Friendship Branding attitude.

- Make return policies clear, easy, and painless. People who return items without a hassle are likely to buy from you again.

- Customers expect and deserve timely delivery. Overestimate the time of delivery if possible. Customers love it when they have been told items will arrive in two weeks and then find it on their doorstep five days later. It feels like they've gotten a bonus treat.

- Make sure there are no hidden charges. Customers shouldn't have to be on the lookout for fine print or get extra charges tacked on when they receive their bill.

- Be flexible. Home shopping channels increased their sales greatly when they allowed shoppers to pay in installments. If you can do that for your customers, or make exceptions to rules for them, they will show their loyalty with increased sales.

- Show your customers you value the relationship more than the sale. Don't disappear after the sale. Maintain the relationship with the following:

Private sales
Special events
Special treatment for best customers
Personal shoppers
Information and education

- Convince your customers that they can count on you, that they are secure every time they deal with you.

A friendship can weather most things and thrive in thin soil; but it needs a little mulch of letters and phone calls and small, silly presents every so often—just to save it from drying out completely.

—Pam Brown

Chapter Eleven

Stage Seven: Building Trust Between You and Your Customer

Trust is the foundation for all relationships. Being trustworthy means always telling the truth, being a good listener, being accessible, and meeting your customers' needs. It takes work. Trust is easy to lose and hard to regain once lost. When customers believe in you, they buy more, they're loyal to you, and they refer friends and colleagues to you. Here are some guidelines to building a firm foundation of trust between you and your customers.

Create an Exclusive Community for Your Customers

Friendship Branding is based on the idea of forming a warm emotional bond with your customer. But the bond needn't be just one-on-one. The more people involved in the bond, the better. That, in fact, is the basis for communities, which are another way of meeting the human need to connect and to belong.

The key here is making your company or your product the heart of the community, the indispensable part around which customers gather. In recent years, no retailer has done this better than Starbucks.

Starbucks shops are not just places to have coffee and bagels. They are breakfast clubs, or break clubs, or Sunday morning gathering places. They are upgraded and institution-alized versions of the old-time general stores or small town hangouts that attract the same local crowd day after day, month after month, year after year.

The community feeling of local hangouts and general stores doesn't usually translate to the next town, or the next state, and surely not to the West Coast, let alone Europe. In the past, every town had its own hangout and each was dif-ferent—different customs, different offerings (donuts, not bagels), different hours, different furniture, different menus, and, of course, different customers.

With Starbucks, every Starbucks is the same. That means you can feel almost as at home in a San Francisco Starbucks as you do in a Chicago Starbucks or a Boston Starbucks. Maybe the faces are new, but when you sit there sipping your latté and munching on your bagel, you know you're among people pretty much like you.

Starbucks is also a kind of oasis when you travel. It's a comfortable place to go and a comfortable place to be. It is a community that radiates friendship.

Such things can happen accidentally—people adopt a store or restaurant or even a product and make it theirs. They build a community around it with little or no urging. But Friendship Branding is not about accidents. It is about the purposeful creation of warm emotional ties between supplier and customer.

That "friendly" feeling is continued in Starbucks advertising. It is friendly and funny and inviting, like the free-standing insert I found in my copy of the *New York Times* recently. Shaped like a brown paper bag, it promises to "lead to outbursts of joy" and "uncontrollable longing"—for Starbucks coffee, of course (see Figure 11.1). Plus, an inside pullout includes a coupon for $1 off (see Figure 11.2).

Starbucks was no accident. The company's management set out to create a chain of coffee shops that were more than just coffee shops; they wanted to create coffee shops that played an important emotional role in the lives of the customers. From the beginning, the chain's creators sought to repeat and build on the elements that made the general store, the local hangout, and the European sidewalk café.

You don't have to have a location to create a community. An excellent example of a company that has created a community of customers is Kirks Folly, a jewelry company that specializes in fantasy-theme pieces with stars and hearts, lucky charms, fairies, angels, wizards, and knights in shining armor. I had the pleasure of visiting the showrooom and speaking at length with Jenniefer Kirk. Kirks Folly has built up a huge following. They offer a free newsletter to buyers and capture their name, address, phone number, and e-mail address. Customers can become members of the Kirks Folly Collectors Family by paying annual dues of $29, which then enables them to purchase exclusive limited edition pieces (see Figure 11.3).

Kirks Folly products are also featured five times a year on QVC. Jenniefer Kirk dresses up in angel costumes and spreads

Figure 11.1 This Starbucks FSI is funny, friendly, and inviting—traits that can describe the brand as well as the entire Starbucks "experience." This fosters customer loyalty by reminding customers what they like about the Starbucks brand, whether they find it in a Starbucks coffee shop or on the grocery store shelf.

Figure 11.2 The FSI for Starbucks Coffee continued with this delightful page that included a $1 coupon toward any variety of coffee.

fairy dust around an elaborate set of white cotton clouds. Jenniefer's brother and two sisters also dress up in costumes and make special appearances throughout the show. It's an image of fantasy, fun, and, most of all, friendship with Jenniefer Kirk and her family.

"I work at having personal relationships with my customers," says Jenniefer Kirk. "I travel a lot, I go to stores and do personal appearances. We send out invitations to all our customers in the area of a store, and we publicize the appearance in our newsletter. Then we go into the store and do a cocktail party or a breakfast. I talk to the customers for about an hour, about anything . . . About the products, about my life, whatever they want to know."

Fans are made to feel like friends and have even been invited to join the Kirk family on a seven-day "fairyland Cruise" to the Caribbean, featuring a Fairyland Ball, a Treasure Chest Boutique, and plenty of "free surprises." On one cruise, a mother planned a big surprise by secretly bringing her daughter's fiancé along. She hid him during the whole cruise until the costume ball, when he came out as Prince Charming (the daughter was dressed as Cinderella). The fiancé came out into the ballroom and asked, "Is there a Cinderella here to try on this slipper?" Then he asked her to marry him. Of course, she said "yes."

The entire Kirk family participates in this event and others like it, and customers come back year after year—not only to have fun in the sun but also to buy more Kirks Folly pieces for their collections (see Figure 11.4).

The "community" aspect of Friendship Branding can be applied to all manner of products. Years ago—don't ask how many—I drove a British sports car, a Triumph. It was a cute, uncomfortable, sporty little car. But one of its charms was

Figure 11.3 Kirks Folly builds loyalty by creating an exclusive club for customers—the Collectors Family—that entitles members to purchase limited edition pieces.

Figure 11.4 The whole Kirk family participates in fantasy events that customers enjoy—dressing up in costumes, dancing at a ball, and, of course, wearing their Kirks Folly jewelry.

whenever you passed another Triumph on the road, you blinked your headlights and the other driver blinked back.

Why the blinking? Well, you were members of the same community. You both knew what it was like to try to put up the balky convertible top when rain threatened. You both knew how hard it was to keep snow from coming through the gaps between the glass and the fabric. You both knew what it was like to have a big truck drive close behind. You both were familiar with the dash-it-all freedom that came from stuffing yourself into the cramped little car and risking your life against vehicles five times your size.

Certain other cars inspired similar communities (early BMWs, MGs, and certain other relatively rare, special interest vehicles). These automakers probably didn't have anything to do with this kind of community feeling. It most likely happened spontaneously.

American carmakers have tried to generate this community feeling for years, with occasionally moderate successes (Corvettes, Mustangs, and Thunderbirds come to mind, and I'm sure there was community feeling among the owners of Stanley Steamers and the first Model T's). But Saturn is the first U.S. manufacturer to truly build a community around its cars. From the moment it first appeared on the scene, Saturn told us it was "a different kind of car company," by which it meant that it was personal, real, and friendly. I must admit I was pleasantly surprised by this branding approach. I anticipated a high-tech image, a kind of updated America-can-do-it-we're-just-as-good-as-Japan-or-even-better look. Instead, I was told that the people building these cars were just like me and, in fact, that they thought about me when they were building them.

Since Saturn first showed up in the showrooms, the company has capitalized—literally—on that approach. I'm especially impressed by the way it talks not only to buyers but also to dealers. I love the company social events and the invitations to owners to visit the plant, where they're given the "one of the guys" kind of treatment, rather than some fawning and phony red carpet treatment.

To my mind, this is what Friendship Branding is all about. It's about a company—and its employees—not only identifying with its customers but also letting them know it, time and again, in as many ways as possible. The company even asks customers to tell them about their experiences with Saturn cars, as shown by the letters they reprint in a series of ads. Does Saturn want to sell cars? Of course it does—but it also wants to befriend the buyers . . . and their families . . . and their friends. This is the road to customer loyalty.

When you're creating an exclusive community for your best customers, don't make it so exclusive that it can never grow. Instead, look for ways to expand it, but without diluting the impression of exclusivity.

Here's one way: Hold a special sale for your best customers, but invite them to bring one guest, who can also take advantage of the sale prices. "Any friend of yours," you could say, "is a friend of ours," and "Anyone in your family is automatically part of *our* family." But don't let them bring more than one guest, otherwise the event is no longer exclusive.

Make Your Best Customers Feel Special

What happens when you stop treating a friend as someone special? Well, eventually, he or she actually stops *being* special. The relationship regresses back into an acquaintance-ship, with bittersweet memories of closeness lost.

In fact, when you cross paths with someone you've been close to—but aren't anymore—there's an inevitable awkward-ness. You tend to treat each other with kid gloves. You're wary of each other. There's none of the naturalness ordinary acquaintances have with each other.

The same is true of the relationship between buyers and sellers, between suppliers and their customers. Once the rela-tionship—or, it is hoped, the friendship—has been established, neglecting it is worse than never making it in the first place.

Imagine this scenario and you'll see what I mean:

You run a woman's clothing store, and you want to broaden your customer base. So you hire a new, younger, trendier buyer and take on a new line of clothing that's hipper than you've ever carried before. And you promote it.

Pretty soon, you start noticing a significant change in your customer demographics. You're still getting your regulars, but now you're also attracting a good-sized crowd of younger women—new and additional customers. They become new regulars, and the volume starts going up.

A few months later, sales figures level, then fall. You can't figure out what's going on. Finally, comes the dawn. Your reg-ulars from before the trendy days are slowly vanishing.

After a few moments of panic, you decide you have to do something to win them back. So you go through your cus-tomer list and do a special mailing, announcing a special sale for your best customers.

The sale comes and few of them show up. Feeling neg-lected, they've found other stores to patronize. They're gone forever.

Even when it comes to branding, friendship can't be a sometime thing. Customers must never feel neglected. They should be frequently reminded that as far as you're concerned, they're special. They're friends.

It is this concept that brought about frequent flyer programs. It's hard to imagine a more cleverly conceived loyalty program. Even Southwest Airlines, the airline with low, low prices and no meals or frills, offers a frequent flyer program. They don't count miles; they count numbers of trips. After you take eight roundtrip flights on Southwest, you get one free roundtrip ticket to anywhere Southwest flies.

And there's Continental's One Pass Program, which is one of the most successful. At the Bronze level, you get to accumulate points toward free tickets, which is enough for you to make the effort to fly Continental instead of its competitors.

But that's not where the One Pass Program ends. If you fly Continental often enough, you are promoted to a new level, the Silver Elite level, where you get even more frequent flyer mile credits—for the same trips. And it gets higher yet for the Gold Elite and, finally, the Platinum Elite levels.

And frequent flyer miles aren't all you get. Depending on how many miles you've accumulated, and what level you've reached, you get free upgrades to first class, put on priority waiting lists, confirmed reservations *even when a flight is sold out*, priority service, priority baggage handling, priority seating, even priority boarding privileges.

Also, as a One Pass member, you get unexpected discounts on car rentals and hotels, as well as surprise flight upgrades.

With all that, Continental could do more. I'd like it if One Pass and the other frequent flyer programs had a somewhat different tone to them—more personal, more friendly, less a matter of simple accounting. Frequent flyer programs are certainly very effective ways to build customer loyalty, but they could be even more effective if they were friendlier and more personalized.

The frequent flyer idea—the better a customer, the bigger the discount—is hardly new. For all I know, Greek olive growers in Plato's time gave buyers one free bucketful for every ten buckets of olives they bought. And my parents—probably yours' too—carefully saved S & H Green Stamps. But the frequent purchase discount is an especially easy Friendship Branding idea to implement, almost whatever the business.

For instance, Enfamil, the baby formula manufacturer, awards customers points according to how many proofs of purchase they save up. Customers can send away for gifts such as a powdered milk container or the *Peter Rabbit* board book.

And the Quality Paperback Book Club (among others) uses a similar technique. Every time you buy a book from them, you earn a certain number of points. These points allow you to get more books from the club at no additional cost.

Even high-end stores have rewards programs—high-end rewards programs. For instance, if you spend $10,000 at Saks Fifth Avenue, you get a merchandise certificate for 6 percent of the amount spent, plus special lunches and parties. If you spend $250,000 at Bergdorf Goodman, you get a ten-day wine-tasting cruise through Burgundy. And if you spend $1 million (or more) at Neiman Marcus stores, you get a free Jaguar or one million American Airlines frequent flyer miles.

But customers don't have to spend a million dollars to appreciate getting rewards. One respondent to the Geller Branding Survey wrote:

> I am constantly getting advance sale coupons from Today's Man. They have good monetary value, and I appreciate the $50 coupon I get for every $500 I spend on their house card. They also have excellent service and help me pick suits quickly and get out (a typical male desire)!

Another respondent wrote:

> I have been buying Volvos and Saabs for the past 16 years, and the dealership has actually taken the time to get to know me and my family. We never have to pay for small repairs or for towing. And we all get birthday and holiday greeting cards. It's a great way to do business.

I've seen the rewards technique used by hotel chains, booksellers, department stores, boutiques, gasoline stations, car washes, even video rental stores. In fact, if you don't have some variation working to reward your best customers and to keep them loyal, you're missing a good bet.

Customer loyalty programs are very powerful when it comes to building long-term customer loyalty. But they are a two-way street. They require a long-term commitment from the companies that use them. They can't simply be scrapped when a new CEO takes over or when a company decides to try a different strategy.

Halting a rewards program or materially reducing the rewards it offers is a sure-fire route to customer rebellion.

Changes in frequent flyer programs have triggered lawsuits that pitted customers against airlines, which is definitely not the way to win customer loyalty.

But here's a suggestion for making those customer rewards programs even more effective: Seal the friendship by occasionally and *unexpectedly* giving extra credits, or accepting nine credits when ten are required. The customer will be genuinely grateful and will feel truly special.

I had an uncle in the furniture business who had a positive genius for making his customers feel special. And it didn't matter who they were, what they were buying, or how much they were spending. Occasionally, I'd get the opportunity to watch him work his magic.

I was in his store one day when a young couple walked in. My uncle walked up to greet them, smiling broadly. "Good morning," he said. "How can I help you?"

"We'd like to look at couches," said the young man.

"Sure thing," my uncle said. "Say, I don't think I've seen you in here before."

"We just got married," said the young woman.

"Ah," said my uncle. "Well, we have a policy here. Newlywed couples get a 15 percent discount off anything in the store, plus a throw rug of their choice."

Needless to say, the couple bought a couch at my uncle's store. They also bought a chair, two end tables, a coffee table, and two lamps. And I'm willing to bet the next time they needed furniture, it never even occurred to them to go elsewhere.

"But how many customers are newlyweds?" you ask. That's missing the point. You can *always* find a way to make a customer feel special.

"You're an old customer, and we want to express our appreciation. That's why I'm going to give you 15 percent off on anything in the store."

"You're a new customer, and we want you to come back to . . ."

"You're from the suburbs, and I want to show my appreciation for your coming so far . . ."

"You're a single parent, and I know it's hard to make ends meet, so . . ."

"You're a couple with children, and I know how hard it is to make ends meet . . ."

"Your parents are customers, so we're going to give you the best customer discount . . ."

"Your friends sent you? Well, if you're friends of a customer, you get the friends' discount . . ."

I once discussed this technique with my uncle, who told me plenty of people had been his personal customers not just for years or decades but for generations. They kept coming back because he always made them feel special. He made them feel like friends.

Plenty of other ways exist to make your good customers feel special. Rolls Royce puts on banquets and fox hunts at English castles, for both old customers and potential new customers. This creates an elite community of people with similar tastes and lifestyles, with Rolls Royce at the center. By the way, the full line of Rolls Royce automobiles is always on display at these events. The message is subtle but unavoidable: If you want to be a member of this community, you'd better own a Rolls.

Of course, invitations to fox hunts might not be right for your customers, but there are many other less extravagant but very effective ways to make them feel special.

Here are even more ways to make your customers feel special:

- Hold an exclusive after-hours sale for best customers only, with special discounts. You can serve wine and appetizers or beer and pretzels, depending on your customers.
- Offer a private fashion show with top models—for your best customers only.
- Send an invitation to your best customers asking them to come to your TV/hi-fi store to see an unreleased movie (or the Big Fight) on high-definition TV, complete with popcorn and slippers.
- Have a special showing, perhaps of an unreleased film, at a local movie house or theater, which you've rented for the occasion.
- Give a Christmas or birthday gift. Best customers deserve something out of the ordinary, and giving them a Christmas or birthday present is definitely unusual. But don't skimp. The better the present, the greater the loyalty you can expect.
- Add something to the box whenever you ship merchandise to good customers. Amazon.com always adds a pack or two of post-it notes. Yes, they say Amazon.com, but who cares. They're just as useful as the yellow kind. And when the customer is a really good customer, Amazon.com ships him or her an insulated plastic mug. They don't make a big deal of this—no announcement that it's coming, no long-winded expressions of gratitude, just an attractive and useful gift—a surprise.

The Difference Between Gifts and Business Transactions

The point of making a customer feel special is to help create that warm emotional bond between you, your company, your products or your services, and the customer. You want to build a friendship, or at least the closest thing to a friendship that can exist in what is basically a commercial relationship.

I want to repeat that word: *Friendship.* If you don't keep that in mind, you may not win your customers' loyalty no matter how many goodies you shower on them. If you forget friendship, your customer loyalty programs will seem like *business transactions*, not genuine expressions of gratitude.

When you spend good money for something and you don't get what you paid for, you have every reason to be annoyed. But when someone *gives* you something you weren't expecting, you can't help feeling grateful, even if the present isn't exactly what you've been dreaming about.

What's the difference between a customer loyalty award that feels like a business transaction and one that feels like a gift? Accounting. When friends give each other gifts, they do it out of gratitude or affection, not to keep the ledger balanced. (And if the gift giving is really a matter of ledger balancing, that may be a sign that *friendship* isn't exactly the right word to describe the relationship.)

Of course, businesses can't eliminate accounting when it comes to best customer awards or special privileges. Some sort of criteria must be applied, which means that a certain amount of accounting is unavoidable. And some customers, I know, enjoy watching their frequent flyer miles or proofs of purchase accumulate. It's kind of like watching your portfolio appreciate.

But once an award is won, all talk of points or miles should cease. From that moment on, what the customer gets should feel more like a gift than an award. It should be delivered with pleasure. It should be presented in as personal a way as possible. It should be remembered after the fact.

For example, airline magazines could feature a column called "How I Used My Frequent Flyer Miles," written by passengers with interesting stories (who could earn extra mileage points if their stories are chosen). Or, even more radical, an airline might call a customer, after he takes the trip he won with frequent flyer mileage, to ask how it went, hear vacation stories, and maybe suggest another destination for next time.

Just imagine that telephone call:

"Who was that on the phone, dear?"

"United Airlines. They wanted to know if we had a good time in San Francisco, and they're sending us an auto rental discount coupon we can use to get away for a weekend this winter."

Wouldn't that kind of treatment go a long way toward building that warm emotional bond?

Dealing with the Disloyal Customer

What in the world is a disloyal customer? He or she is someone who buys not only from you but also from your competitor, or stops buying from you and starts buying from someone else.

When a customer stops buying from you, it's time to get back in touch. There is nothing more heartwarming than hearing from a friend you've lost touch with. Even if you're not in constant communication, a note once in a while is greatly appreciated.

At lunch one day, Markus Wilhelm, president and CEO of Doubleday Direct Inc., said that his most successful direct mail piece is a catalog that shows a cartoon-like pussycat holding a bunch of flowers (see Figure 11.5). Inside the catalog, the cat, holding a box of candies, says, "We'll beg . . ." and then offers six books for $1 (see Figure 11.6). This is a catalog that reactivates club members worldwide. It's simple, yet it's a sentiment everyone recognizes.

Figure 11.5   This charming catalog is Doubleday's most successful direct mail piece!

Figure 11.6   Who can resist a cat (with flowers) who begs you to renew your membership? Not many people can, according to Doubleday.

So, how do you deal with a disloyal customer? You treat her like a good customer. You treat her like a friend. And maybe she'll become both.

Don't Try to Trick or Manipulate Your Customers

The other day, I got a strange envelope in the mail—exactly the size and shape of one of those photo envelopes you get at the drugstore. In fact, the phrase "photos enclosed, do not bend" was stamped on both sides of the envelope.

The envelope had a glassine window, through which I could see my name and address, evidently scribbled by hand. On one side, where you'd expect to find the price, a big red arrow marked "price" ran all the way down the side and pointed to $0.00, which at first glance seemed like a good thing.

And you know those check boxes you find on film development envelopes? They were here too, with check marks in prints, 35 mm, glossy, and 4 × 6. Also printed on the envelope were several sets of numbers and some bar codes.

I didn't recall sending photos out to be developed, so I was quite perplexed by this piece of mail. Finally, I opened it and pulled out a small yellow folder with three photographs.

Photograph number one, a colorful number, showed three smiling people, two men and a woman, along with a large check from a major publishing company with my name on it, telling me I'd won $21 million.

Could this be?

I looked at the second picture—a whole group of people, holding a sign welcoming me, "our newest $21 million winner." The third picture was a color shot of a fancy table setting. A card near the plate said "Winners' Luncheon, Guest of Honor, Lois Geller."

You've got to give these guys credit. They have an unlimited imagination—and unlimited gall as well. They had gotten my attention with a direct mail piece unlike any I'd seen before, and believe me, I've seen thousands.

So how did I feel, looking at these three pictures, and the yellow folder with its phony check boxes and my name printed on everything? I felt irritated. I felt manipulated. I felt tricked. What I did not feel was that a friend had sent me a letter.

Oh, the trick may work. Once. You may be able to unload a mountain of merchandise. This publisher has done okay with the technique. But you won't have a second shot at it. And you'll have lost any chance to win your customer's loyalty, or friendship.

Okay, another example: A few years ago, I walked into one of those "discount" electronics stores that can be found throughout midtown Manhattan. I was in the market for a little tape recorder, and I was lured inside by the lurid red and black "Going Out of Business," "Last Few Days," and "Below Wholesale Prices" signs plastered over the windows, through which you could usually see a cornucopia of cameras, computers, tape players, hi-fi equipment, and similar electronic toys.

As I walked into the store, I was greeted by raucous music, broken paper boxes scattered about, and strips of newspaper covering the floor. I was also greeted by three different salesmen, who looked me up and down to estimate the value of my clothing, and by reflection, the number of greenbacks they might pry out of me.

I browsed for a bit among the electronic goodies in the showcases, checking the prices of a few tape recorders I was familiar with. They were priced about the same as others I had seen at similar stores. All the while, I purposefully showed no special interest in any one thing, so as not to provoke an attack from the salespeople.

But I was intrigued by the strips of newspaper on the floor. They didn't seem to be packing. They weren't the leavings of a platoon of newspaper readers. In fact, their presence was a complete mystery.

Glancing at my purse to make sure it was securely closed, I approached one of the salesmen and smiled. "Why all the newspaper strips on the floor?" I asked, pointing.

He glanced at the floor, then back up at me. Then he gave me a conspiratorial wink. "It's atmosphere," he confided.

"Nice touch," I said.

"Thanks."

I smiled and walked out, slowly, pleased that I'd successfully escaped the distress sale atmosphere that was supposed to convince me the prices were so low that if I bought something, I'd practically be getting it free.

Of course, that electronics shop in midtown Manhattan wasn't interested in developing customer loyalty. With 15 million people in the Metropolitan area and who knows how many tourists, that store felt no need to respect its customers, much less befriend them.

But many other merchants—merchants who cannot draw from an unlimited number of potential customers—spend their days and nights thinking up tricks such as phony sales, endless essential accessories, seconds or old models passed off as perfect or new, discounts that expire if not used immediately, 50-percent-off sales that are actually two-for-one deals, worthless prizes and extras ("Get a free diamond ring with your purchase," which is accurate, but only if you have microscopic vision), threats of coming price increases—the list is endless.

These tricks are practiced not only in direct mail and retail stores but also in catalogs. About a year ago, a large electronics mail-order company mailed me a catalog filled with some of the lowest prices I'd ever seen. I had my American Express card in my hand and was reaching for the phone when I noticed that each low-priced item carried a line in tiny print that I hadn't noticed earlier. The tiny print read: factory reconditioned.

"What's that?" you say. Well, let me make it perfectly clear: FACTORY RECONDITIONED. That's another way of saying "repaired," which is another way of saying "used, broken, returned, and fixed." No wonder it was cheap. And no wonder that I no longer open this company's catalogs.

Don't Deceive Your Customers

Many companies have behaved like the ones I've described—deceptively. That behavior is the exact opposite of Friendship Branding.

The tobacco industry is a great example of this type of deception. Cigarettes, as told to us in a thousand different ways, taste good. Cool people smoke. It failed to tell us that smokers also died, and at appalling rates, from cancer, heart disease, emphysema, and a dozen other diseases. However, the tobacco industry wasn't worried about the loyalty of its customers. That little problem was taken care of pharmacologically, with nicotine.

What should the tobacco industry have done, you ask? Should it have released the research it conducted between

1940 and 1960 that proved the connection between smoking and cancer? I say "yes"—absolutely. That research should have been released to the public as soon as the results were in.

What would have happened to the tobacco industry as a result? It might have crashed and burned. The stockholders—and, more significantly, the corporate officers and the company's thousands of employees—would have been hurt. But millions of human beings who died before their time would have lived full lives.

What the tobacco industry did when it withheld that research was lie to its customers. That may work for a while, but when the lie is uncovered—and it usually is—the liars will never be trusted again. They will have lost the confidence of the public and their customers—past, present, and potential. The same goes for untruthful bragging and exaggerating.

Don't Abandon Your Friends

My friend Samuel recently bought a computer. Sam's no expert on the subject, so he did a lot of comparison shopping before purchasing, studying ads for different brands in computer magazines. He read articles from *Consumer Reports*. He talked to friends and "techies" he knew. And they all ultimately recommended one particular brand. The impression he came away with was overwhelmingly positive. So far so good.

When Sam called the recommended company, the salesperson was extremely helpful. He asked questions about what Sam wanted, why he needed a new computer, and exactly how he would be using it. He recommended certain upgrades and told Sam he didn't need others. The customer service person had a sense of humor and made Sam feel comfortable while making a large purchase. He said he would fax Sam a quote for everything he wanted, with all the components listed and the total system cost. The list was faxed within minutes. Sam liked this salesperson and trusted him. He felt good about his buying decision.

The computer arrived. It was packaged carefully. There were even easy-to-understand set-up instructions. Sam felt it was a great brand.

And then, silence.

No note accompanied Sam's purchase. Nothing that said, "Congratulations! You made a good choice," or "Glad to have you as our customer." There was no phone call or e-mail asking if everything had arrived safely, not even any encouragement to buy other products from this company—nothing to say, "This could be the start of a wonderful friendship."

In fact, Sam has never heard from this company again. And even though he likes his computer, he feels let down. Abandoned.

This brand missed a perfect opportunity to "marry" a customer to them and build brand loyalty. At the moment Sam received his computer, he was ready to continue the relationship. But this company has made it quite clear it's not interested in investing any time or effort to cement that bond. All the positive Friendship Branding steps the company took before the sale were shown to be nothing more than slick seduction. It worked, this once. Now my friend is telling everyone he knows how he's been disappointed. The company could have been friendlier, thanked him for his purchase, then offered him add-ons, accessories, screen cleaners, computer books, and even upgrades.

The Total Customer Continuum

That brand dropped the ball because it did not complete the "Total Customer Continuum" or TCC. The TCC means that the customer is treated like a friend from the very first contact, past delivery, and into the future of the relationship. Each contact a person has with your brand creates an impression, good or bad, and has the possibility of cementing a friendship or chasing an acquaintance away. That means that every customer should have continuous positive experiences with your brand.

There is an old saying that goes "You never get a second chance to make a first impression." I'm not convinced that's totally true, but I do know that you'll forgive even your best of friends only so often. Too many mistakes and the relationship is over. Your friends need to know they can count on you all the time: when they see you on the street, when they send you a letter or an e-mail, when they talk to you on the phone, when they're invited to your house. Your customers must be able to rely on your brand in the same ways.

A positive first impression can be ruined when your customer receives merchandise stuffed into a brown plastic bag. That bag sends the customer the message that you don't really care. If, on the other hand, the package is carefully packed and beautifully wrapped, the message that is transmitted on the Customer Continuum is that you go the extra mile.

To show you how the Total Customer Continuum works, I've "incorporated" the following fictitious computer company, Edward's Electronics, which rates highly on the Customer Continuum scale. Here's how they do it.

Advertising

Their advertisements, like their products, are geared toward individual computer buyers rather than large corporate customers. The ads are simple and straightforward. The ads also have the human touch—they feature the company's owner, Mr. Edwards, in a variety of work-at-home settings. Prices are competitive. They differentiate themselves with their reputation for helpful salespeople and excellent service.

Promotion

Edwards uses a variety of promotions, including discounts for buying a computer and a printer or purchases of more than one computer. They offer in-store demonstrations, led by company employees who are experts in both hardware and software problems. They also offer free workshops in how to create a newsletter, how to use a spreadsheet, and how to find what you need on the Internet. These are offered at lunchtime and in the evening to make them convenient for their customers.

Public Relations

The company owner, Anthony Edwards, is well known to the public. He has been profiled in several magazines and newspapers and often appears on news programs as an industry expert. Also, he sponsors several charity events and has established the Edwards Foundation to Computerize the World. When you buy a new Edwards computer, the company will pick up your old one free of charge, refurbish it if necessary (whether it's an Edwards or not), and donate it to low-income schools in the United States and abroad. Edwards is also well known as a chocolate lover and often makes his own chocolate treats at home (which have been featured in several gourmet magazines). The chocolate is given away in the store and to inner-city children at holiday times.

Direct Marketing

Mailings from Edwards include a short customer survey to past customers. The survey asks what types of equipment they already own and what they may be shopping for in the future. They also want to know what consumers like and dislike about computers they already own (Edwards or others) and how Edwards can improve its products and service. Edwards sends its buyers a quarterly newsletter that tells them about new applications, about buyers and their home offices, upgrade ideas, and interesting Web sites.

Outbound Telemarketing

Operators spend several weeks learning communications skills along with product information. They are taught to be friendly, to listen to customers, to answer questions, and to deviate from their script if necessary. Since most of the telemarketing is to sell other products to current customers, operators are encouraged to ask customers if they are having any problems with their current equipment or if they have any suggestions for product development.

Inbound Telemarketing

These operators go through the same training as the ones in outbound direct marketing. The company hires enough operators so that no customer has to spend more than two minutes on hold. It is Edwards policy. If you wait more than two minutes, you receive a box of Edwards chocolates to "sweeten" the wait.

Retail

The company has retail stores around the country, and customers are encouraged to come in, sit down at the computer, and stay there for as long as it takes to get the feel of each Edwards model. Salespeople are courteous and knowledgeable. The company has developed a unique selling aid: It's a recorded tour (similar to the kind they have available in museums) of the various computer configurations that are available. When you come into the store, you get a Walkman with a tape that tells you about each computer as you pass by. If you need help at any time, you press a button on the Walkman, and a salesperson will come to assist you.

Internet

The company's Internet site was designed by the same people who designed its advertising campaign, so it has the same tone and personality. Potential customers can easily design their own system configurations and find out how much the system will cost. Shipping and handling charges are clearly stated. There is an e-mail address and an "800" number listed for anyone with questions.

Delivery

The company sends customers an e-mail to let them know the computer has been shipped. It includes the name of the shipping carrier and the tracking number, in case the package doesn't arrive in a timely fashion. The computer comes sturdily packaged and includes simple, clear instructions for setting up the system. It also includes a letter from Anthony Edwards, welcoming customers to the Edwards Electronics family, and offering a 15 percent discount on their next order. And customers are pleased to find that they have also been sent a chocolate candy in the shape of a computer, made from Anthony Edwards' own recipe.

Customer Service

One week after delivery, a customer service representative calls you to find out if everything arrived all right, if you had any problems with setup, and if you have any questions. They also ask if there is anything else you would like to purchase.

Creating trust between you and your customers is one of the most important results of Friendship Branding. And once customers feel safe with you, they will become lifelong friends. Remember . . . the key to Friendship Branding is attitude. Maintaining a secure, caring, and considerate relationship with your customers will assure them that your company is really looking out for them.

Chapter Summary

- Create an exclusive community for your customers. Fill the basic human need people have to connect and belong. Think about the examples in the chapter and examples from your own experiences. What could you incorporate for your own company's customers?

- Make your best customers feel special. Like the saying goes, "It's the thought that counts." Your best customers will feel really warmly toward your company when you acknowledge them and their patronage. It shows them that you really do value them. Be aware of the difference between gifts and business transactions.

- There are ways to handle the disloyal customer. Usually when our friends don't talk to us, it's because we did something (unintentionally to be sure) that offended or upset them. It's the same with customers. To win them back, we need to try and find out what we did wrong and make it right. If we can't uncover the specifics, we should just continue to treat them well and hope they give us another chance.

- Never try to trick or manipulate your customers. Shoppers have more savvy than ever, and you'll only lose them in the end. Take an inventory of your products and services to find out if there is any product or service that's received complaints? Now's a good time to revisit these "problem spots" and make things right.

- Don't abandon your friends. Never take friends or customers for granted. Nothing is worse than being ignored by a friend. How do customers perceive your company after they've made a purchase? What else could you do to cement bonds with customers?

- Establishing a Total Customer Continuum for lasting relationships. This means treating customers like friends at every stage of the process—across advertising, promotion, public relations, direct marketing, telemarketing, retail, the Internet, delivery, and customer service channels.

- Make sure your customers know that as far as you're concerned, they'll always be special to you.

We cannot tell the precise moment when friendship is formed. As in filling a vessel drop by drop, there is at last a drop, which makes it run over. So in a series of kindness there is, at last, one which makes the heart run over.

—James Boswell

Chapter Twelve

Stage Eight: Creating Friendships That Last

Just as we can't take our friends for granted, we should never take our customers for granted. We have to be willing to do our part to develop friendships that stand the test of time.

Don't Forget about Me

I have a friend name Marilyn. Both Marilyn and I lead very busy lives. She lives in Atlanta, and I live in New York. I think about her all the time. But I have to admit, I'm not such a great correspondent. I keep meaning to call or write, but somehow . . . I don't. Then after a while, I think such a long time has gone by that I'm embarrassed to call.

Thank goodness Marilyn doesn't feel that way. When a few months have gone by, she always gets on the phone and gives me a ring. "Lois," she says, "it's been too long. How are you doing?" I love to hear from her, and as soon as we get on the phone, it's as if no time at all has passed. Even though I may not speak to Marilyn for months at a time, I consider her one of my best friends.

Brands should treat customers the way Marilyn treats me. She doesn't wait for me to call. She doesn't get insulted when I don't call her. She just picks up the phone and calls me. Marilyn doesn't threaten when she calls. She doesn't say, "You haven't called me in three months. If you don't call me next week, our friendship is over." No. She knows I'm busy and that I mean to call her (and I do call her, too—it's just that she calls me more often). I appreciate her friendship even more because I know I can count on her to be there for me whether or not we speak frequently.

I can't say that I can count on many of the companies I deal with to be there for me. If I don't make an effort to contact them (which means if I don't buy something), I never hear a word from them. They seem to forget about me altogether. Or if they do remember me, it's to "threaten" me with the loss of their friendship. I always have to laugh when I get a catalog that says in big letters on the front, "This could be the last catalog you receive from us," or "This could be your last catalog. Order today." Do they think I'm scared of receiving one less catalog in the mail? Do they give me any reason to "order today," anything that would be a special incentive? No. All they do is threaten, and I don't see this "threat" as a friendly gesture.

Here at Mason & Geller, we have a list of "sleeping clients." These are people we haven't done business with for a while. Every few months I give them a call. I just call to chat. It's not a sales pitch; it's simply a "how are you?" Sometimes that's where the conversation ends. But many times a client will say, "Lois, how nice to hear from you. As a matter of fact, I'm glad you called. I've been thinking about launching a new marketing campaign, and I could sure use your help."

If I don't call, I send them a handwritten note on stationery we had made that features the faces of all our staff (see Figure 12.1). It reminds our clients that the people in our office miss the people in theirs. And often I find that even if these clients don't have any immediate business for us, they're constantly referring new customers our way.

Figure 12.1   This note card shows the "human" side of Mason & Geller to clients and prospects.

I would never just let an old customer fade away. I understand that they may have to leave for a while, but I want to be sure they know we're here for them whenever they want to come back.

Your customers are your company's most valuable assets. They not only pay for your goods and services but also, if you listen to them, tell you how you can get them to spend even more. Industry estimates tell us it costs anywhere from three to seven times more to get a new customer than to retain an old one. Yet many of us spend most of our marketing time and money trying to attract new prospects. If you spend more of your marketing budget on retention, and less on new business, your profits will immediately increase.

Develop Customer Retention

The secret to successful real estate is location, location, location. The secret to successful Friendship Branding is retention, retention, retention. Developing customer retention means being committed to earning every buyer's long-term loyalty. The very first purchase a customer makes is an overture toward friendship; it is a signal that there is a strong possibility for an ongoing relationship between the customer and you. That customer has taken the first step, and it's up to you to continue the relationship. Once you lose communication with a customer, it's very hard to rekindle it.

Most people would agree that the task of satisfying today's customer is more demanding than ever. Competition in every industry has swelled dramatically, due to product parity and to a wider variety of businesses offering similar services. When Amazon.com first started, for example, only those people selling books worried about the new competitor. Now, just about every kind of retailer has to be aware of what this e-marketing giant is doing. Today, all varieties of marketers are jostling with one another to offer better service, more products, and lower prices. Brands once accustomed to relatively secure customer relationships are now fighting to maintain a healthy share of the market.

Should your company go out and get new customers, or are you better off concentrating on keeping your current customers and increasing the number of dollars they spend with you? For the past several decades, new customer acquisition has driven the thinking of many brands. But many of those same brands are now realizing that developing long-term partnerships with customers is a better way to ensure long-term profits.

In fact, according to an article by Jeff Resnick in *Marketing Review* (December 1996), "Research shows that companies that excel in creating loyal customers can command prices from four to seven percent higher than less able competitors and generate up to three times more profit."

Who are these loyal customers? According to Resnick, they are "repeat customers who buy more of the [products or] services you offer, who convince their friends to do the same, and who pump up profits." So why do so many brands seem to have such difficulty understanding the importance of customer retention?

It could be that customer retention is not always easy. It requires a systematic, companywide commitment. It must become the basic philosophy behind your brand, and it must be understood and embraced by every single employee, from the chairman of the board, to the president, to the telemarketers, to the shipping clerks.

The Curriculum Approach

The best way to make customers and friends for a lifetime is to keep in touch with them. It takes a strong effort to retain hard-won business relationships—and that means more than just saying "thank you" each time a customer buys again. That's important, but it's also important to realize that the times between purchases are critical to keeping customers.

That's where the curriculum approach comes in. That means that you continue to talk to them over time—before they buy from you and after they buy from you so that they'll continue to buy from you. Suppose, for instance, a pharmaceutical company comes out with a new drug for treating osteoporosis, which it advertises in various magazines directed toward women and the aging population. I see this ad and ask my doctor about it. He prescribes the drug for me. After he prescribes it, the drug company gets my name from the pharmacy and sends me a newsletter with information and education about osteoporosis. They continue to send me quarterly newsletters, supplemented by occasional other mailings, such as a form I can fill out month by month showing my compliance with the drug and recommending daily and weekly exercise goals.

The outcome of this approach is that I will probably continue to take this drug for a much longer time than someone who has received no communication at all.

It's not just drug companies that follow this approach. Mercedes has developed a curriculum approach for its customers. A buyer's purchase decision is immediately reinforced with a thank-you gift from the company. On Valentine's Day, the buyer receives another gift and card that says, "We love all our Mercedes drivers." The relationship continues with periodic communications. Eventually, the company sends a notice that the new Mercedes models are coming up. They give their current customers a "sneak peak" at them before anybody else gets a chance to see them. It makes customers feel part of an exclusive club (and encourages them to trade in their old models for new ones, of course).

If your brand isn't quite as upscale as Mercedes, the curriculum approach is still the best way to go. You might not communicate as often or as lavishly as Mercedes, but the principle remains the same.

Deceptive Communications

You do have to be careful about the communications you send, however. They must be in keeping with your overall image and tone, be relevant to the particular customer, and be honest and straightforward. It's all right if the communication is, or contains, sales-related materials, as long as it is honestly stated.

I got a mailing recently from a credit card company that did not follow this rule. It was just before the holidays, and the mailing stated in huge letters, "We have a holiday gift for you." The letter (four pages long) went on to say that because I was such a valued customer, I could have my choice of a full-size calendar-diary (embossed with my initials in gold) or a pocket diary (also embossed) for only $3.95, the cost of shipping and handling. If I wanted, I could have both pieces for only $4.95.

The offer was tempting—until I realized that in the middle of a paragraph in the middle of this long letter was a sentence that told me that this was a negative option offer and that by ordering one or both of these books, I would automatically get a new one every year for only $49.95 (billed directly to the credit card, of course)! The credit card company was betting on the fact that I wouldn't read the whole letter and wouldn't realize I was signing up for a life-time supply of these diaries.

There's nothing wrong with negative option programs. Many companies, such as book and record clubs, use them successfully. But customers know what they're getting into. Let's face it; the offer from the credit card company was not a free gift to a valued customer. This letter was designed to deceive. This is not the type of communication that fosters friendship. At the end of the next year, when thousands of loyal customers get their new diaries—and an unexpected bill for $49.95—the company is going to lose many of its friends. And it will be very difficult to regain them. Once you violate your customers' trust, it's almost impossible to get it back again.

Keeping in mind that honesty is the best policy, there are many other ways to keep communication lines open with your customers. Let your customers know what's going on with your brand. Introduce them to people in your company—it's much easier for customers to form bonds with real people than with a brand name. For example, if the president of your company has a new baby, or takes a white-water rafting vaca-tion, or gets an honorary degree from his or her alma mater, send out an announcement! Let all of the president's (or the vice president's, or any of the employee's) "friends" in on the good news.

One of my favorite methods of ongoing communication is to offer customers education. This is something I do with my own agency. I like to invite clients to my office for lunch or after-work wine and cheese and have a guest speaker give a brief talk. The speaker is someone who is an expert in a field that is of interest to both my clients and to prospects (whom I also invite so that they can see how happy my current clients are). For instance, we recently had a party with special guest Andrea Neirenberg (see Figure 12.2). She spoke about networking, and we invited everyone to practice this skill after her talk. Clients and prospects had a good time and a chance to make some new connections.

Mason & Geller cordially invites you
to a Wine and Cheese party
and a breath of fresh air
out on our deck
May 25th, 1999
5:30 to 8:30 p.m.

Special guest, Andrea Nierenberg
CEO – The Nierenberg Group
will speak on
"Following Up – Post Convention
Networking"
(starting at 6:15 p.m.)

RSVP: Sharyn Kolberg
212-697-4477

Figure 12.2 Mason & Geller invites clients and prospects to "educational" parties as a service and a friendship builder.

How to Develop a Customer Retention Program

The key to customer retention is building targeted customer relationships. To do that, you've got to identify your most profitable customers, understand what they value most about your brand, and put procedures in place to keep these loyal customers satisfied. There are several questions you can ask yourself to help develop an effective customer retention program:

- How do I identify which customers are most valuable? Many companies fail to differentiate between customer segments, treating them equally despite major differences in profitability. You can find your best customers by scanning your database for RFM (recency, frequency, and monetary, as discussed in Chapter 5).

- What do customers value most about this brand? Many companies assume that people are most interested in price. This often results in companies making offers that are based on low prices—in other words, they try to buy their customers' loyalty. But, as the Geller Branding Survey discovered, price is not customers' highest priority in forming loyalty to a brand. The number one reason is "consistent quality," followed by "customer service"—and then "price." While price is important to consumers, low cost alone won't keep them coming back for more.

- Do all my customers want the same things? Study your database to find out what products different customers are buying. Knowing who is buying what allows you to develop offers specifically for certain customers. Why waste precious marketing and promotion dollars selling a product to everyone in your entire database when only a small percentage may actually want that product?

- What do my customers expect from this brand? Do they want luxury and impeccable, personalized service? Do they want a huge selection? Do they expect sales personnel to be extremely knowledge-able? The only way you can be sure you're meeting your customers' expectations is to know what they are. This may mean conducting customer surveys or focus groups to discover exactly what your customers do expect—and how well you're doing at meeting those expectations.

- What differentiates my brand from others like it? Find out what the perceived differences are—ask your customers to compare your brand to that of your competitors. You may be surprised to find that the differences are not what you thought—your customers might have other opinions. If so, you need to capitalize on those perceived differences to stay ahead of your competitors.

- Are my retention programs reactive or proactive? Many brands concentrate on winning back customers who have recently defected. While this is important, it is more important to establish an ongoing, proactive relationship with your customers to stop them from defecting in the first place.

Fifteen Great Ideas for "Friendly" Customer Retention

Here are some great ideas for implementing your own customer retention programs, Friendship Branding style:

1. *Know thy customers.* Build a marketing database and segment the file so you know which customers are buying from you and how much they are spending. Know the number of individual units each customer is buying as well as the dollar volume. Also know when your customers are buying. If everyone seems to be buying in October or November, you can surmise that they're buying for holiday gift giving. If buying is seasonal, you can send reminders to your customers saying, "You bought three gift orders from us last year at this time. Is there anything we can do to make your gift giving easier this year?" Your customers will appreciate anything you do to make the buying process easier for them.

2. *Devise new ways to reward your best customers.* Segment your database and tie your marketing frequency into the dollar amount the customer spends and their overall profitability potential. Pick your best customers and talk to them more often. Send them unexpected gifts. Only consider a loyalty program like a frequent flyer (or frequent buyer) program if you're willing to make a long-term commitment to it. You can't give your customers a special membership program and then take it away after a few months because the administration is too costly or too time consuming. If you're going to create a rewards program, be sure it is cost efficient.

3. *Close the loop in your marketing programs*. Improve your tracking and keep fine-tuning your programs. Find out which customers are marginal and try to improve their buying record. Offer them quantity discounts on items similar to those they've already bought. Send them a survey to find out why they stopped buying, and then give them a special premium for filling out the questionnaire.

4. *Maximize the personalization of offers*. Design offers that are targeted directly to your customers. Once you know what people buy from you, you can make offers specific to their buying habits. Suppose I have been buying vitamin E from you every three months for several years. You should send me a targeted offer for a discount on my next purchase of vitamin E, along with the opportunity to participate in an automatic shipment program. You can also build one-on-one relationships by having as much information as possible about each customer. Then, if a customer calls to reorder, say, linens for the bedroom, your telephone representative could say, "Would you like to order the same size linens you ordered last time?" Providing such personal services makes customers believe they are so important to you that you know what they need before they do.

5. *Identify the timing and frequency of customer promotions*. Study the information from your database and modify your unique selling proposition to each of your customer groups. Test your mailings over time. If you are sending mailings ten times year and getting a low response, try increasing or decreasing the frequency, then measure the lift (or decline) in response. Companies often continue

the same mailing schedule they've followed for years simply because "that's the way it's always been done." What worked in the past may not be working now. There may be more cost-efficient mailing schedules you can follow to get a better response.

6. *Keep your customer retention programs human.* Remember you are dealing person-to-person, not company-to-person. Everything that you mail to your customers and prospects should sound like it's coming from a human being, not from some inanimate company. And you should be using the same "voice" in all your communications. It's not just a matter of consistency. It's a matter of establishing and maintaining a distinctive personality. Any mail that I get from Mrs. Smith's Children Clothing Company, for instance, should reflect the personality of the company. It's that quirky "Mrs. Smith" personality that first attracted your customers, and it is what will keep them interested.

7. *Do the unexpected.* Unfortunately, customers today are almost surprised when they are treated well. People expect to get what they pay for and nothing else. So if they are treated well, they are going to stick around and keep buying from you. Staples customers are used to receiving Dividend$ (credit toward future purchases based on how much they spend). But just before Christmas, Staples offered customers extra savings on store, catalog, and online purchases.

Even small touches like thank-you notes and birthday cards really work well toward overall customer retention. It's easy to send thank-you notes—they can be built into when you send the bill or be sent out automatically after the customer has paid. And believe it or not, birthday cards can mean a lot to customers. I'll always remember the audience member at one of my seminars who said that she loved to get birthday cards but that the only card she got last year was from her oil burner man—and now she would never change oil companies.

8. *Reinforce your customers' purchasing behavior.* There have been many studies conducted on post-purchasing behavior, and ways to make your customers happy about the purchase they just made. Many car dealerships send their customers a letter after they buy a car, telling the customer what a good choice he made, how terrific his new car is, and that they know he'll get a lot of enjoyment from it. This is an effective customer retention technique because the smarter you make your customers feel about having bought your product, the more likely they are to come back and buy from you again.

   This is especially effective with large purchases, although it works for smaller purchases as well. And it can be extremely effective in business-to-business situations—simply because it is so rarely done. Companies are sometimes afraid to send out this after-sale component because they think it gives customers an opportunity to complain. But if there's something to complain about, you should know about it so that you can improve your product or your service.

9. *Deliver excellent customer service.* Customers expect that when they have a problem, they will be treated with respect and that their problems will be a high priority to your employees. Customers have the right to return items that they deem unsatisfactory. Studies have proven that a

customer who has a problem that is solved by customer service has a high likelihood of buying from you again. The catalog industry has known this for years. The customer will usually minimize the problem and spread the word about how quickly and efficiently it was solved.

Everyone dreads returning things they've bought, so when they have a pleasant experience in this situation, they tend to let other people know. However, if they have a bad experience, they tell even more people. Customer service is an even more important component of customer retention in direct marketing or Internet marketing, because people are buying from you on faith. They don't get the chance to try on your merchandise, or take a test drive, or see the purchases at all, except in a small photo in a catalog or direct mail package or on the computer screen. They don't get to check out our publications before they subscribe to them. So they must have the right to change their mind about a purchase, and to be treated well when they do.

10. *Utilize retail and catalog synergies.* Use multiple distribution channels to improve customer retention. Many retailers have extensive mail-order operations (e.g., Bloomingdale's, Saks, and Williams-Sonoma). The retail channel can feed catalog sales and vice versa. Today, more and more catalogers (e.g., Hold Everything, Sharper Image, and Eddie Bauer) are opening retail outlets. And now, of course, there's the Internet that links them both. The synergies of all three venues make it easy for customers to shop with a company whether they're at home or at the mall. The more ways you have for a customer to shop with you, the better the chances they will remain loyal.

11. *Use partnerships to build customer retention.* Partnerships build value for your customers. When Citibank Visa partnered with American Airlines for frequent flyer miles, the two companies both built customer loyalty and retention. But you don't have to be American Airlines or Citibank to take advantage of partnering opportunities. Partnership can work for all kinds of companies. A children's clothing company, for instance, might find a toy company with similar product quality and values and create increased profit and customer retention for both companies.

12. *Utilize online marketing.* Maximize the ability for customers to place orders quickly and cost effectively. Every single transaction in e-commerce today can provide an opportunity for customer retention. It allows you to provide personalized service on demand. By simply asking Internet users to click on certain preferences, you can provide totally customized offerings. For example, Web surfers can visit QVC's site, then click on "My Mailing List," where QVC offers customers the ability to "choose from hot QVC topics such as recipes from In the Kitchen with Bob"; then QVC offers e-mail shoppers relevant news on a regular basis. It also offers "My Style Advisor": Customers complete an online questionnaire and receive a Style Advisor Profile, personalized for body line, face shape, and coloring; then QVC makes appropriate fashion and jewelry recommendations.

If customers have a problem with a product, they should be able to go online and get it solved. The Internet provides an immediacy of customer service that's never been possible before. The better that service is, the more customers will return to your site again and again.

13. *Reward customers for referrals.* Ask present customers for referrals, people they know who might be interested in your company. First of all, they will be flattered to be asked their opinion. Second, it is an effective customer retention device, because once they've recommended you to a friend, they will feel a special bond—both with you and with their friend—and continue to buy from you.

14. *Train your telemarketers to represent your company.* They are the voice of your brand. Part of your customer retention strategy should be to make sure that your Telephone Service Representatives truly represent your company. That means they must have extensive product knowledge. You should screen telemarketers yourself—listen to them answering calls. If possible, give them samples of your product so that when customers ask questions, they can answer them intelligently. And, of course, they should be as pleasant and polite as you would be if you were answering the phone yourself.

15. *Deliver a high-quality, high-value product.* This is the most important customer retention technique of all. Make sure that your product or service is everything you promised it would be, in every way, from its construction to it delivery. There should be no discrepancy between the copy I read or the ad I see and the product I buy.

Customer retention programs do more than get people to spend more money. They bring you closer to your customers. Your customers feel like you're doing something special just for them. And you are.

Now that you know how to develop a friendly brand, understand the Friendship Branding attitude, and are comfortable with Friendship Branding techniques, how can you start implementing Friendship Branding in your company? I know you want to get started, so let's look at the eleven steps in the next chapter.

Chapter Summary

- Creating friendships that last takes work. The way to achieve it is to be committed to earning every buyer's long-term loyalty. Think about companies that you are loyal to and why?

- Communicate with your customers on a regular basis. The best way to make customers and keep friends is to stay in touch. Consider all your options and then commit to an approach.

- Never be deceptive or misleading. That's no way to treat friends.

- Follow these steps to develop a customer retention program:

  Identify which customers are most valuable.
  Find out what customers value about your brand.
  Determine what customers buy and what customers want.
  Find out what customers expect from your brand.
  Determine whether your retention programs should be reactive or proactive.

- Apply the fifteen great ideas for "Friendly" customer retention.

Friends are treasures.
—Horace Bruns

Chapter Thirteen

Eleven Steps to Getting Started with Friendship Branding

By now, I think you should have a good understanding of Friendship Branding and the effect it can have on customer loyalty. If you've been reading, my bet is you're sold.

But I'll also bet you're asking yourself how in the world you can implement this branding concept. I want to be frank with you: It won't be easy. To do it, you have to overcome the indifference, greed, even hostility that are part of human nature.

I know you want steps, so here are the steps to implementing Friendship Branding in your organization.

1. Buy into the Idea Yourself

If you have doubts, you'll never convince anyone else in your organization to accept the idea. Work to understand, at the most profound possible level, that what you do—whatever it is—is not just on your behalf but on the behalf of others, people who need or want your goods or services, people whose lives will be better in some way because of what you provide.

2. Bring the Senior Members of Your Organization into the Fold

You can't do it all yourself. Friendship Branding is not just a way of doing business; it is a calling. And if some people in your organization are with you only halfheartedly, you are just as likely to fail at Friendship Branding as you are to succeed.

3. Spread the Word Through the Entire Organization

About now, you're probably thinking "mission statement." And yes, Friendship Branding deserves to be built into your mission statement. But if your mission statement is just lip service to nice-sounding principles, it won't work. It has to become an integral part of what you stand for.

4. Hold Meetings on the Idea of Friendship Branding

Have meetings for the production team, the marketing team, and the salespeople, both separately and together. Everyone in your organization must not only understand the idea and its benefits to the company and to themselves as individuals but also know how to put it into practice.

5. Create the Post of "Chief of Customer Relationships"

Make this person responsible for coming up with Friendship Branding ideas that make sense for your company, for solving customer problems to their satisfaction, and for helping various company units apply Friendship Branding principles whenever possible.

Once staff and employees have truly adopted the idea of Friendship Branding, start putting it to work in sales, advertising, and credit departments. Make the principles of Friendship Branding an integral part of your company's activities.

6. Create the Structures That Make Friendship Branding a Reality

Make company policies customer friendly. Work out how you can best treat good customers, how you can recognize their patronage and make them feel appreciated.

7. Work Hard to Personalize All of Your Customer Contacts

De-emphasize the institutional aspects of your company. Put your best face—and I do mean face—forward.

8. Create a "Customers' Bill of Rights"

Write out what you are dedicated to providing—for example, merchandise at a fair price, fast and courteous repairs, money-back guarantees.

9. Improve Communication

Create mechanisms to improve communication with customers in both directions, that is, ways customers can talk to you and ways you can talk to your customers.

10. Tell the World What You're Doing

In addition to letting your employees and your customers in on your new techniques, also inform your suppliers, partners, subsidiaries, and the general public. The object is to commit your company and everyone in it to a new and better way of treating customers.

11. Don't Conclude That the Job Is Done Once You've Followed the First Eleven Steps

Put yourself and your employees through a refresher course at least once a year. Make sure new employees get the word during orientation. Reread the book from time to time and pass it around. (I wouldn't even mind if you bought several copies and gave them to the people who would benefit most.)

Chapter Summary

- To make it work, you need to really believe in the power of Friendship Branding, and you need to work to get buy-in from key members of your organization.

- You need to make sure the concept and applications of Friendship Branding are clearly understood through your organization.

- You need a single individual who is accountable for making sure that your company works toward Friendship Branding.

- Complete steps one through eleven and then revisit the principles of Friendship Branding at least once a year.

Conclusion

As a Final Word . . .

Friendship Branding is a technique you can use to build long-term relationships with your customers and to begin having a relationship with prospects. It is best to think always about your brand in terms of being a real friend to your customers. So, the same traits that we like so well in others, are the ones we should use in developing our brand.

Begin to be a "Brand Watcher." What does Nike do that makes the brand always fresh and new to its customers? Why do people around the world want Nike shoes, clothing, and so forth? Maybe they're like me . . . and they aspire to be a great athlete like Michael Jordan or Andre Agassi. My athletic prowess is virtually nonexistent. In fact, walking across an icy street in New York without falling on my face is a feat for me. But somehow, when I go to my aerobics class wearing my big bulky Nikes, I think, and believe, that having them on my feet gives me a chance to make it through an entire hour gracefully. I like a brand that says "just do it."

Brands that try to foist themselves on me will never be my friend. MCI does that when I am having dinner at night and their telemarketer calls and insists on telling me about their newest offer. It would be great if, after I told her that I was having dinner, she would ask about a convenient time to speak to me. I would tell her, and we'd set up a date. That would make MCI a Friendship Brand for me.

But instead of asking for a convenient time to call, they alienate me by hanging up. Would you hang up on a friend when they told you they were in the middle of dinner? No, courtesy would prevail and there would be a follow-up call. Take note MCI; it is a good branding technique for you.

Friendship Branding involves a long-term commitment by your company and all the employees that work there. This is tough to achieve today, because management turnover is much faster than ever before, and when a new manager comes aboard, she usually wants to change things—especially the company brand.

That is what happened at Weight Watchers. They had been using two chubby cartoon ladies—Brenda and Elaine—to give a voice to the millions of Weight Watcher members struggling to lose those pounds. Then management changed, and the new group wanted Sarah Ferguson as their spokesperson. So, the brand was inconsistent. That confuses customers. It is as if your friend were transformed from an everyday cartoon lady to the Duchess of York overnight. That might have brought in some new members, but I am not sure how their loyal customers reacted. It was very abrupt. It might have been good to have a transition, for instance have the cartoon characters introducing Sarah Ferguson.

Friendship Branding means you have to always be innovative and yet consistent with your brand. The idea is to keep your customers interested in you by being creative, unique, quirky—having personality. If we want to consider a dull product, think about simple coffee beans. They cost about $1 a pound, which is about a penny a cup. If I buy a cup in the coffee shop here in New York, it costs me about seventy-five cents. If I go over to Starbucks and order it with some hot foamy milk and cinnamon, and relax in the nice shop and people watch—that cup costs about $3.00.

If I order some fabulous coffee from Gevalia, they send me a coffeemaker and a pound of different flavored coffee each month. It's a great treat, having that variety to select from, on a cold Sunday morning in New York City. So, I won't balk if it costs me $1.75 a cup.

And there are times when I have the opportunity to go to a five-star restaurant, where the ambience is just beautiful, the waiters are attentive and instructive, to order a cup of coffee. It tastes about the same as some of the others, but the atmosphere and the experience are so great . . . I don't mind the $5 tab for the coffee.

The bottom line is that I will buy a cup of coffee at the coffee shop, but I will also at times pay more for the service of receiving it at my home. I will pay more for the experience I have in the five-star restaurant. I will pay more for that coffee when I feel that it is being served to me by a friend, be it a kind waitress, a charming owner, or a cute young high school kid raising money for a band trip.

The point is that people will pay a premium for a product or service that they perceive as special. In the case of the cup of coffee, I'll pay anywhere from $.75 to $5.00.

In Friendship Branding, think outside the box. Remember the case of the waste disposal products and how their management put a humorous twist to their products by offering them through the New Pig catalog.

Consider Walt Disney's vision of Disney World—the amusement park that he created. It is not just rides; it is such a marvelous experience that every kid (and their parents) want to go there. The exhibits are fascinating, the streets are fun, the cartoon characters are friendly, and the place is clean.

Think about that delicious brand, Krispy Kreme. Sure, they make great donuts, and we love them. And they give out Krispy Kreme hats (this year my son and daughter-in-law wore them to a Christmas dinner). They are fun, and they make you smile. You can also buy their donuts to use as a fund-raiser. They sell them to you at a discount, and you walk away knowing that they are a Friendship Brand.

Friendship Brands do unexpected things. There is a chain of restaurants called the Cheesecake Factory; they are usually located in malls. Since they always draw a huge crowd, they give each group a beeper. Then they ask you to go shopping and come back when they beep you. It is a very friendly thing to do. They heap on generous portions of delicious food, serve you in a dimly lit restaurant in enormous comfortable chairs, and feature their cheese cake extraordinaire—they are a Friendship Brand. They think about you, the customer.

That is what I want you to do always. Think about your customers first. They are your friends, so treat them that way. And test different breakthrough ideas to keep them interested. Most of all, make every experience they have with your company a good one. And if for whatever reason it isn't, make sure that the problem is remedied quickly.

Adopt a policy whereby you want to keep every customer you currently have. They are important to you.

When you begin testing these Friendship Branding steps, you will see a change not only in your business but also in your employees and in yourself. It is a lot easier to treat people as friends, than otherwise.

After you have begun building your Brand, please let me know how it is working for you. You can e-mail me, fax me, or send me the form at the end of this book.

Good Luck!
Lois K. Geller

Appendix A

Every Business Can Use Friendship Branding

Let's assume that you've got your Friendship Branding attitude in place and tightly fastened. What can you do to show your customers they've got a friend in the front office . . . and in the back office . . . and on the design team . . . and on the production floor . . . and on the sales floor?

Specific Opportunities

Here are some specific ideas for specific types of businesses. If necessary, translate them to suit your own situation.

Department Store

- Put a face on your company. It's difficult to relate to a store, especially because so many are so similar. Try to connect someone's face or personality with your store. It could be a real person connected to the store (the founder, perhaps), a spokesperson (a well-known personality like Rosie O'Donnell for Kmart), or a cartoon character. For instance, Marshalls stores invented "Marsha," a character who appears in all their advertising and commercials. She's cute and funny, and she sets Marshalls apart from other off-price discount stores.
- Keep track of customers. Technology is making it easier and easier to keep track of all customers, not just those who have store credit cards. For instance, suppose you were a chain of athletic shoe stores, and you were implementing a campaign in which customers who bought three pairs of shoes got a fourth

pair free. You could use a simple sticker or punch card system. But in order to capture their names for your database, you could have people fill out their names and addresses at the store, and then give each customer a card with a unique bar code. That way, whenever they bought a pair of shoes, they could present the card to the cashier, who could then scan it into a storewide system. At the end of the promotion, you'd have a large database you could use for direct mail purposes and special offers.

- Use direct mail to build store traffic. Rent lists of zip codes within a particular radius of the store, then mail these prospects a special incentive to come in and shop with you. This gives you a chance to introduce yourself to potential customers in your area who might not otherwise know you exist.
- Have in-store promotions. These are a wonderful way to extend your brand. You could have people come to your store to speak (like Barnes & Noble does), or you could give away collectible premiums (the way McDonald's does). These are great store traffic builders, and they help people to remember your brand.
- Offer "best customer" sales. What could be friendlier than inviting your best customers to a sale that the general public doesn't even know about?
- Create "best customer" personal representatives. Best customers deserve special, or personal, treatment when they come to shop. So assign them a personal shopper who can get to know them, their tastes, their needs, even their spending patterns.
- Offer "friends and family" sales. If you want to bring in more loyal customers, empower your best customers to bring their friends and family in and give them discounts and special treatments. "Every friend of yours is a friend of ours," you might say.
- Offer "share the bounty" discounts. When business is good, let your best customers benefit too, with special sales and discounts.
- Give unexpected rewards. It's been said that those who give to charity anonymously have purer motives than those who want recognition of their generosity. It's the same thing with rewards: The unexpected ones are much more powerful than those a

customer feels he or she deserves. The rewards needn't be expensive to be effective, just unexpected.

- Keep a record of purchases, sizes, and preferences. If you're going to make friends with your best customers and create that warm emotional bond that keeps them coming back year after year, you're going to have to remember who they are, the sizes they wear, and the clothing preferences they have. This is a perfect job for a computer database. You can even give customers a clothing inventory form they can fill out and return to you for entry in your database; then, when they come in, they can shop intelligently—or, to put it another way, your salespeople can serve them intelligently and very personally.

- Give each customer a personal salesperson. Ideally, your good customers should be handled by the same salesperson each time they visit so that a relationship can be established and so that the salesperson can better cater to his or her customer's tastes and needs.

- Send out now-in-stock notices and/or discount notices. When, with the aid of the store's computerized database, the salesperson knows his or her customer well enough, the customer can be sent (or phoned) in-stock notices regarding items he or she might like. "I know how much you like suede," the salesperson might say. "Well, we've just gotten a shipment of suede jackets in, and I think you'll find one that you love. Come in this week, and I can give you the 10 percent preferred customer discount."

- Offer a gift registry. Gift registries aren't just for weddings anymore. They're a wonderful way for families and friends to tell each other what they'd like at Christmas, on birthdays, and as no-special-reason gifts. Your store should have one and promote it. A gift registry came in handy in one store when a customer picked out more items than she could afford and the salesperson suggested listing the extra items on the gift registry.

- Offer a "tie one on—on us" reward program. When a customer makes a big purchase—a suit, for instance—your store can reward him on the spot, with the "tie one on—on us" reward program.

Smaller purchases can get the "sock-it-to me" reward, and larger ones the "I pant for you" reward.

Hardware Superstore

- Have design and planning services. When it comes to hardware and home projects, customers may need help. For these folks, professional, on-site advice is friendship at its finest.
- Offer off-site help and advice. Nothing is too good for your best customers, including having someone available to actually visit their site and offer suggestions.
- Give instructional classes. The do-it-yourself craze has been a bonanza for hardware and lumber stores. But the percentage of homeowners who actually participate is small. Free instructional classes for good customers, even for potential customers, could do a lot to build your base and win loyalty.
- Offer printed and video instruction materials. This is the same idea as instructional classes, but on a smaller scale. It's just another way of offering what do-it-yourself homeowners yearn for most: help in making their dreams come true.
- Have on hand project personal representatives. When a good customer is building a backyard screened porch, he shouldn't have to go from department to department, selecting the materials he thinks are necessary and dealing with several different salespeople. Instead, a single expert should take him on, as a kind of client, and provide all the services he needs. And if they become friends in the process, so much the better.
- Offer an after-hours advice line. When do customers build decks? They build decks on weekends and in the early evening hours— when most stores are closed. And all too often, they quickly confront problems that bring their project to a halt. The solution is an after-hours help line manned by a real person. Who do you go to when you need help? You go to a friend. Stores should volunteer to be that friend.
- Hold contests and giveaways to build a database. Like department stores, hardware superstores should build a database.

You could do that by asking customers to fill out an entry form for an in-store contest. Then, several times a day, hold a drawing to give away a book on home improvement, or a hammer, or a can of paint. Then use the names and addresses of the participants to build a database and start mailing these customers special offers.

Fund-raising

- Make contributors feel good about donations. I know people are supposed to contribute out of the goodness of their hearts, but sometimes they need a little more incentive. Always send a thank-you note, no matter what the size of the donation. And let donors know exactly what their money is being used for.
- Invite your "golden tier" donors to special events or give them special privileges. People who give more should be entitled to more. That way, a $500 donor will say, "Oh, for only another $500 I'm entitled to . . ." If you can't spend money on rewarding donors, reward with status; for example, list their names in a program or on a plaque on your wall.

Professional Service (Legal, Medical, Tax Prep, Etc.)

- Avoid jargon and similar mumbo jumbo. Nothing is less customer friendly than language the customer can't understand or has to think about twice. And yet professionals love to spout such stuff because they think it makes them look like they know more than their clients. Thing is, their clients already accept that; otherwise they'd be doing their own legal work, or taxes, or surgery. All that jargon does is distance client and service provider from each other. Use it only when there's no other choice.
- Make people available after hours. The need for professional services knows nothing about normal business hours. Sometimes it can wait, but very often the need is intense, even desperate, and must be filled immediately. For that reason, one of the friendliest things a professional service firm can do is make its people available *after* hours.

Restaurant (Franchise and Otherwise)

- Have a "best customer" club. Good customers should have special privileges at a restaurant. They should get preferential reservations, preferential seating, preferential service, perhaps even preferential menus and wine lists.
- Offer a "birthday meal on us." Do you want your customers to routinely choose your restaurant when they want to go some place special? Then remember their special times—their birthdays and anniversaries, for instance. One free meal will win you a score of paid-for visits.
- Remember your best customers. Hostesses should be required to call good customers by name. Their favorite dishes and wine selections should be noted in the kitchen, and this information should be used by the waitperson. Friends remember that kind of information about friends . . . and it's a compliment your best customers won't forget.
- Throw "best customer" parties. Invite a bunch of your regular customers to a special this-time-it's-on-the-house dinner. "Any friend of yours should be a friend of ours, too," the invitation might read.
- Invite your customers to taste new recipes. Have the chef come out (again, it puts a face to your brand) and pass around a tray with small portions of a new recipe you're thinking of adding to the menu. Diners will be flattered to be asked for their opinion.

Service Station

- Have a reward system. Regular customers should be recognized. They're the lifeblood of service station business. These rewards could consist of free winter tire installation, free oil changes, or other free services, all earned by a certain level of patronage.
- Give unexpected rewards. Here's an easy one: Whenever a customer leaves his car for the day for repairs or servicing, wash it for him. Have it clean when he comes to pick it up. Here's another easy one: Offer pickup and delivery services for your best customers. That can be a tremendous convenience.

- Revive the free map practice. There was a time when any driver could get a free map at a service station. These were printed by the gasoline companies themselves. But that service has disappeared, along with routinely getting your windshield washed and your oil checked. That's why reviving the free map practice would be so appreciated by your best customers.
- Offer after-hours help. The most important thing a friend can do for another friend is help him (or her) when help is needed. This is especially true for service stations, because most people are really helpless when something goes wrong with their car, and because the inconvenience can be serious. This service need not be available to casual or occasional customers; it could be presented (perhaps in the form of an after-hours business card) to your best customers, perhaps as a surprise gift.
- Notify car owners when their registrations or inspections must be renewed. This gives service stations an excellent opportunity to be customer friendly. Create a database that compiles that information for your best customers and notify them by postcard when their time has come, in the same way dentists notify you that it's time for a cleaning, or vets inform you that your pet needs this year's shots.

Bank or Brokerage House

- Encourage children to start saving. When I was young, there was a bank called the Seaman's Bank for Savings. They used to give out little banks to encourage children to start saving their pennies. Banks do nothing these days to encourage anyone to save. A great way to extend your brand to the community would be to hold seminars for elementary school children about how to start saving money.
- Offer education seminars. Adults need savings tips as well. There are many areas of finance—even such elementary topics as opening an account—that would draw customers to free seminars.
- Stop unfriendly banking practices. When a colleague of mine went to open an account recently, she was told that she could

get a no-fee account if she promised *not* to use the tellers at the bank. She could do everything using the ATM and online banking. If she wanted to use a teller, she'd have to pay extra. How do you expect customers to form a relationship with ATMs and computers? Why would anyone remain loyal for such non-service? Surely my colleague will change banks as soon as one makes her a better offer—with better service.

- Put on a human face—deinstitutionalize. The bank officers should be available at all times. They should know the names of the bank's best customers and introduce themselves to new customers. Keep a coffee urn in the central lobby, along with cookies. Dress up the bank for the holidays. Encourage bank employees to engage in community activities by having bank teams and bank help days.
- Offer after-hours banking. Your best customers should be able to do their banking at their convenience, not yours. After they reach a certain level of deposits, loans, and checking account balances, they should be given access to some type of (limited) after-hours banking.

Auto Dealer
- Get involved with the community. Auto dealers sometimes have a shady reputation (deserved or not). You can counteract that by sponsoring a Little League team, giving awards to community leaders, or giving away scholarships. Or have your team form a volunteer corps that visits the elderly and infirm in hospitals and nursing homes.
- Have a single point of contact. For many customers, an auto dealership houses two separate businesses: new (or used) car sales and car service. From a Friendship Branding point of view, this is not a good situation. It complicates the dealer/customer relationship. Here's an alternate idea: Have a single point of contact. For as long as the customer owns the car, establish the relationship between the customer and the salesperson as the primary one. The salesperson reminds the customer when

servicing is necessary and supervises the repairs. The customer has a single point of contact who is definitely on her side, since the salesperson is responsible for making good on his initial promises about quality and reliability.

- Have the owner make contact with repeat customers. At an auto dealership, when a customer buys his second car . . . or his third . . . or his fourth . . . he deserves a personal thanks from the owner of the dealership. He needs to be treated—as much as possible—as a friend, not simply a wallet.

- Throw "best (or new) customer" parties. One way to build a warm emotional bond between a company and its customers is to hold social events—picnics, for instance, or barbecues, or nights at the local roller rink—in which the company staff mixes informally with the customers. You can invite just your best customers and your top staff to the party, or new customers, or all customers and every member of the staff. The object is to have fun and bond.

- Address the single most annoying aspect of car ownership: service and maintenance. Audi began offering free maintenance in 1987, in response to the news reports that its vehicles were accelerating suddenly, without warning. In 1993, Volkswagen, concerned that its Mexican assembly plants were not building quality vehicles, joined this movement. South Korean carmaker Daewoo has also begun offering free maintenance, in an effort to establish itself in the U.S. marketplace. Recently, both BMW and Mercedes have offered free maintenance for the length of the vehicle warranty, from two to five years. That saves customers anywhere from $800 to $1,000. But I don't think the savings is the point, except in the sense that people get weary of writing checks to car dealers for every little thing. The point is that taking care of this problem is just about the friendliest thing a car manufacturer can do for its customers. It creates goodwill every time the customer comes in for service. It also exposes customers to the latest models. And it is a fine example of Friendship Branding.

Communications Service (Phone, Cell Phone, Cable TV, Internet Service Provider)

- Have a single point of contact. Nothing is more annoying than being transferred from one department to another to another, and having to tell your story again and again and again. How can you eliminate this problem by applying the principles of Friendship Branding? Give the customer a single point of contact—at least each time he or she makes a call. Charge the person who answers the call to stay with the customer until the problem has been solved or the situation resolved.

- Offer an immediate response to technical problems. Communications companies are sorely tempted to offer as little technical support as possible—to give customers a recorded announcement with "frequently asked questions" or to ask them to leave their names and numbers for later callback, or to put them on hold long enough to go out for lunch. Every time any of these things happen, even the most placid customer can be infuriated. If a communications company is to truly act toward customers in a friendly way, it must recognize that customers are disabled by communications problems and that they need *immediate* and competent service.

- Compensate customers for loss of service, even if the failure is brief. If your network goes down, for whatever reason, you're obligated to refund any charges for that period. Don't wait until the customer demands it. Make the refund without being asked. This is not just being friendly; it's being fair.

- Give advance notice of new services or service changes. If you're going to have to raise rates, let your customers know as soon as *you* know. Explain in convincing detail why you must do this. If you don't do this, your customers will find out through the newspapers or by word of mouth, and they won't get any satisfactory explanation for the increased charges. The result is customer anger, not customer loyalty. The same goes for new services. Be the first to provide the good news. Make it come from one friend to another.

• Encourage cell phone etiquette. Be the "refined" cell phone company and include a guide to cell phone etiquette with every
phone you sell. It would position you as someone who cares
about your customers (e.g., talk about safety issues of using the
phone in your car). It would do us all a favor.

Catalog

• Provide reduced (or free) shipping for best customers. Shipping
fees are customers' biggest gripe. And why not? They usually wipe
out any discount that your company gives. They put a price on the
convenience of catalog or online shopping, and the price doesn't
seem small. You probably can't afford to absorb the shipping costs
for everyone, but you can't afford not to for your best customers.
You could even make this part of your point reward system; offer
free shipping for a year once a customer passes a certain level.

• Provide free shipping for returns. If a customer has to return something—whatever the reason—your company has somehow failed to
satisfy her. She shouldn't have to pay for the privilege of returning
the merchandise. Your company should do that, and it should
make the return as simple as possible. Remember, it's not the individual sale that matters—it's the customer. If you make her happy,
if you win her loyalty, she'll give you sale after sale for years.

The Internet

• Change your site weekly. The Internet is a visual medium. Visitors
want something different almost every time they visit.

• Identify your visitors and welcome them back personally. Have
people register the first time they visit your site. Then when they
return, they should see something that says, "Welcome back, Lois
Geller [or your customer's name]."

• Make your site easy to navigate. Be sure all pages are clearly
labeled and that it is easy to order from you. Speed is what the
Internet is all about, and if customers have to spend more than
a few minutes trying to figure out what to do next, they'll click
themselves out of your site.

- Make your site interactive. You need to present more than banner ads to establish a brand presence on the Web. As the Internet evolves, so does the brand experience. Advertising Age's Business Marketing Online quotes Bob Dorf, president of Peppers & Rogers Group/Marketing 1to1 of Stamford, Connecticut, as saying, "With its interactive possibilities, the web puts the onus on the marketer to build relationships with potential customers. The branding power of a site really hinges on its ability to engage an individual customer or business customer in repeated interaction."

Small Retail Store (Bookstore, Boutique, Card Shop, Etc.)

- The owner should always or usually be on the sales floor, known, available, and friendly. One of the most important advantages a small retail operation has over the chain stores is that the storeowner can develop personal relationships with his or her customers. This should be done at every possible opportunity. It is one of the most important ways to cement customer loyalty.
- Salespeople and clerks should be expected to call all good customers by name. Once more, the object here is to be personal—and friendly. The more people in a store that the customer has bonded with, the better the chance he or she will come back again and again.
- Know your customers' wants and needs. That's what "personal" really means, and that's what gives you an advantage over larger, less personal retail operations. If possible, feature customer preferences—show off the dress that the homecoming queen bought at your store. Name sandwiches or other meals after your steady customers. Create customer reading lists so that their friends can see what books they've bought.

Mass Production Manufacturer (Drug Company, Appliance Maker, Home Products Manufacturer, Etc.)

- Provide easy contact—prominent toll-free numbers, Web sites, e-mail—all well staffed. The purpose is to make it absolutely as easy as possible for a customer to contact your company, either

with praise or with a complaint. It creates a communications network that allows communications to flow in both directions. If
you make it hard for your customer to contact you, it won't be
long before she isn't interested in doing business with you anymore, either.

- Take every opportunity to humanize (or deinstitutionalize) the
company. Customers are intimidated by big companies. They're
intimidated by impersonal treatment. They're put off by rules and
regulations that always seem to work against them. There's
nothing about your size or your gross profits that makes customers feel warmly toward you. That comes from knowing and
liking the people they deal with in your company. That comes
from being treated truly well. That comes from trust.

Public Agency (City, State, Federal)

- Have a single point of contact. Nothing is more infuriating—and
time wasting—then to be shuttled from window to window at the
Motor Vehicle Bureau or put on hold and transferred from
person to person to person at OSHA or any other agency. The
solution is a single point of contact.

- Consider users "customers." Very often, government employees
act as though they are annoyed when they have to deal with the
public—even if that's their job. Part of the solution is to convince
them that these people are their *customers*—and can be treated
with friendship and consideration to the benefit of both parties.

- Deinstitutionalize communications and advertising. Very few
human creations are less personal than public agencies. The
result is that people are uncomfortable and put off when dealing
with public agencies. Resentment and distrust rules. People don't
speak well of public agencies, and public agency employees have
to deal with their discomfort. Maybe there's no complete answer
to this problem, but here's something that might help both parties: a sense of humor—and humanity—in agency advertising
and communications, and even between agency employees and
the public.

- Put a human face on the agency. The best way to humanize any institution is to give it a human face. How? Display names and pictures of the agency's officers. Also, display the names and pictures of the employees who come into contact with the public. This is often done, but only in the most formal way possible. It should be done in the most *in*formal way possible. Also, encourage agency participation in all kinds of public events; set up baseball and bowling leagues, or sponsor local charity events, holiday events, parades, and so forth.

I hope you could tell while reading this book that I believe in Friendship Branding with all my heart. My goal is to help you believe in it, too. I want you to know that I am here for you. If you have any questions, write to me, and if I can't supply the answers, I'll help you find them.

If you are willing to make a commitment, to take a chance, to keep Friendship Branding in your mind and in your heart, you will succeed. And that's really what I want.

Appendix B

The Geller Branding Survey

While doing research for this book, I decided to conduct a survey. I asked several hundred people what they looked for when making purchases, what brands they liked and why, and (since my background is in direct marketing) how they felt about catalogs and direct mail.

Most people claim they hate all those catalogs they get in the mail, right? Wrong—at least according to my survey. In fact, no matter how much we might complain about catalogs and "unsolicited mail," more than 51 percent of respondents to my survey said they'd like to receive *more* catalogs.

On the other hand, the survey (which was accurate to plus or minus 4 percent) did confirm the conventional wisdom when it came to shipping costs. On a scale of 1 to 5, with 1 being most important and 5 the least important, poll respondents felt that lower shipping costs were the single most important factor that could improve catalog shopping, rating it an average of 1.9. Good shopper rewards were the next factor that would convince them to order more, with an average of 2.2.

The survey also asked a number of questions about brand loyalty. Respondents ranked advertising dead last in factors that keep them loyal to a particular brand. And if you expected "price" to be the number one reason for loyalty, you'd be wrong. The number one reason was "consistent quality," followed by "customer service"—and then "price."

This survey confirmed what I have long suspected: that customers are especially loyal when they are treated well, when the service they get is unexpectedly generous or personal or speedy.

Index

I'd like to hear from you. So please fill out and return the letter below (attach an additional sheet of paper if necessary).

Dear Lois,

I've just read *Customers for Keeps*, and I'd like some feedback on incorporating these techniques into my organization. My question is:

_____

_____

_____

Can you send me more information about_____

_____?

Please add me to your mailing list for all your free communications.

Name: _____

Company: _____

Title: _____

Street: _____

City:_____ State:_____ Zip:_____

E-mail: _____

Mail to: Lois K. Geller
            Mason & Geller Direct Marketing
            261 Madison Avenue
            18th Floor
            New York, New York 10016

            Phone: (212) 697-4477
            E-mail: *loisgeller@masongeller.com*
            And visit us at *www.masongeller.com*